Ver / Best Wishes / Bob

Mark '03

# THE WAY
# TO LIVERPOOL

Bob Evans

GW00643214

For D'rene,
the Family
and Friends

First published 1999 by Countyvise Limited, 14 Appin Road, Birkenhead, Merseyside, CH41 9HH in conjunction with the author R.A. Evans

Copyright © 1999 R.A. Evans

The right of R.A. Evans to be identified as the author of this work has been asserted by him in accordance with the Copyright, Design and Patents Act 1988.

British Library Cataloguing in Publication Data.
A Catalogue record for this book is available from the British Library.

ISBN 1 901231 14 3

# CONTENTS

The Start................................................................1

The Arrival..............................................................7

Consolidation.........................................................15

Hidden Talent........................................................22

Hard Work.............................................................26

The Three of Us.....................................................32

The Family.............................................................41

Shock Treatment...................................................52

The Way In............................................................57

Settled...................................................................65

Togetherness.........................................................71

Per Ardua..............................................................78

Itchy Feet..............................................................84

Majestas................................................................95

Charlie.................................................................102

Work is Play.........................................................112

Questions.............................................................123

Groundwork.........................................................130

Crossroads...........................................................140

Home...................................................................150

## Foreword by Len Holder

*"Most roads lead men homewards,*
*My road leads me forth .........."*
*John Masefield*

"The Way to Liverpool" is the third book by Bob Evans. This story is told with the same wit and wisdom as the other two, but the message is a more personal one. The first book, "A Dog Collar in the Docks" gives an insight into the lives of seafarers of the River Mersey and the role of the Mersey Mission to Seamen within that community. The second, "Mersey Mariners" explores the history, aims and achievements of the organisations that shared that welfare role. This book describes the aspirations, experiences and decisions that paved Bob's way to Liverpool from an unlikely background in the valleys of South Wales. At each step along the way, he developed skills and gained experience which would be needed later. Whether this was lucky chance or divine guidance, you must decide for yourselves or take Bob's word for it.

When I read "How Green Was My Valley", I wondered whether miners' lives were really so hard. Were mining communities rigidly structured in their social lives as well as at work? In Cwmdare, Bob and his wife D'rene were to endorse many of Richard Llewellyn's visions of society. They learned the place of their church in that society and how to communicate and work with others in difficult situations. They also learned to live with mice! If you want to find out why their valley was cleaner than most, because no coal came out, only miners, you will need to read the rest of the book!

From Cwmdare they moved to Tremorfa which at that time was a "depressed area" without prospect of work for many. What the area needed was inspiration and leadership. An uphill struggle, some progress made with the help of Bob's RAF background and a few willing helpers. More lessons were learned, particularly about young adults. When you read about D'rene's experience with the National Health Service maternity facilities, you realise today's hospital problems are not new.

Thence to Llandaff and a complete culture change. Still with parish responsibilities as well as the higher level ceremonials of the cathedral. Bob introduces us to another mouse, this time working on his behalf to awaken the imagination of children.

Looking for a new challenge Bob, with D'rene and the three children, made his way to Liverpool and a completely new life for them all. It was not straightforward. We learn how close the family came to returning to South Wales. Fortunately for the seafarers of Merseyside they made Liverpool their new home. The rest, as the readers of "Dog Collar in the Docks" will know, is history.

L.A.Holder
Chairman, The Mersey Mission to Seamen

iv

## *Preface.*

An autobiography is a series of coloured snapshots, hopefully in order of time, but more often like life itself full of tangents, laughter, tears and a sense of the ridiculous. Certainly, my memories are not in straight lines, yet in the act of writing there emerged a pattern which proved to be the foundation for the Liverpool years and all this led to the writing of *Dog Collar in the Docks* and *Mersey Mariners*. This book, *The Way to Liverpool,* spells out the first ten years of my ministry (1950 to 1960) and the groundwork for the thirty years work amongst seafarers came alive to me in the telling.

There are so many people to thank. Without D'rene and the family there would have been little motivation to continue or to appear in print. Each member of the tribe made a firm contribution, both reading, advising and correcting the script. D'rene certainly proved to be a mine of memories and an honest critic ... we met at the age of eight in school! Stephen and Brig ... Stephen gave ideas for the cover painting and along with Brigita proof-read with a purpose. Jane and John ... Jane enthused and encouraged, whilst John happily produced a number of proof copies. Martin, Heather and Katy ... Martin read wisely, created his linedrawings and sketches and computerised the lot, Heather read and approved, whilst granddaughter, Katy, said "Go for it, granddad!"

I thank so many friends who have read the manuscript ... too many to name ... who along with others have all given valuable advice. Jill Dagnall, artist and teacher and friend, gently prodded and encouraged my efforts at painting the cover ... she is very patient! Yet again, Captain Len Holder and his wife Ann have been a source of strength and countless cups of coffee. John and Jean Emmerson of Countyvise Limited are not only responsible for the printing and publishing, they have always given friendship and encouragement. However, any blemishes, mistakes, misjudgements and omissions are entirely mine ... with apologies.

It really has been fun to remember with love ... and then say "Thank you to those with whom so much has been shared".

Bob Evans
The tail end of 1999.
Liverpool.

# 1.
# THE START

Parsons are not created in heaven. They emerge from the laity, endowed with all the frailty of man and, with luck, just a little of the divinity expected of them. I was to be one of them. Examinations were completed; so the last term at St. Michael's College in Llandaff was devoted to the nebulous subject called pastoralia. The year was 1950.

It had been a long haul since my boyhood days in Bridgend County Grammar School, a year at Cardiff University, three years winning the war in the R.A.F, another two years back battling for a degree, all topped up with two further years reading, but not entirely understanding theology at St. Michael's College in Llandaff, having my soul tuned and burnished and knees polished and brain suitably washed. Now, apparently, I was ready for the halo to be affixed about my neck.

Euphoria had set in as ordination was just around the corner. The next step would be to wrap on the dog collar and be let loose into the world. I did not feel that I was the answer to a sinner's prayer, but fully realised that at least I would understand his problems. Maybe that would have to do!

Pastoralia is concerned with the work of the parson on his patch. For those two years after finishing my degree at University, my head had been bombarded with theology, which is the study of the nature of God and, as we were assured that God is incomprehensible, not one of us was surprised to find the going a little difficult. But, at last, we were to think about the practical implications of being a parson, the joys, the pitfalls and the absurdities! The Warden of the College was the Reverend Eryl Thomas and, as he had been a Parish Priest for many years, he knew his onions. He had one final term to teach us how to handle the dog collar in the wide, wide world.

In turns, we had to preach a sermon before the other victims in the College. Nothing was more intimidating, but we need not have worried; our bumbling efforts were treated with complete sympathy. How could anyone criticise when he was next into the firing line? The real test was reserved for our first full-time congregation. That was when our problems would become their problems.

All of us had performed in various Parish Churches near our homes, but they had been only one-night stands with no possible retribution and no visible affect on the minuscule congregations, most of whom were fast asleep, extremely old and when awake, somewhat deaf.

"Good night."

"What was the name again?"

"Bob Evans."

"Ah! Yes!"

The name had been noted with no further comment.

They knew that they would never see us again, so they smiled as they disappeared into the night. This was the pre-television era; at least we were a topic for conversation in the hills and valleys of South Wales. We rightly assumed that we could do little harm to their long suffering souls.

A doll was produced. This enabled us to practise baptisms and thus avoid culpable homicide. The nearest that I had ever been to a baby was side-stepping a well aimed pram in the High Street. Each child to me seemed to be a potential monster with a built in design fault, resulting in unfortunate leaks. I had a theological question.

"Do we do total immersion?"

"Only if you drop one!"

It was better not to think about the first live baptism.

That doll had a God-forsaken, battered appearance; it had survived being ham fisted with grace by those who had gone before us. Washed out might better describe it! Faith and observation told me that real babies are natural survivors. They emerge into the world, upside down, out of a pool of water, only to be greeted by a resounding smack from the midwife. They were already conditioned to accept our ministrations and most would ignore us parsons for the rest of their lives.

Academically, we discussed funerals. How could the necessary expertise be taught? Obviously a little more than the ability to push a button in the crematorium would be required. All that I can recall of the advice was ... 'say as little as possible, never offer suggestions, merely allow the next of kin to talk about their loved one.' Almost fifty years on, I can only agree. Just being there is enough. It is of more value to hold the hand than to open the mouth. Above all, never ever say that you understand. That would be the final hurt, as no-one knows the depth of sorrow in others.

The dog collar was about to descend from on high! The final four days were spent in Retreat, leaving no further time for heart searching. That Retreat was not the usual peace and quiet one expects. We experimented with our new dog collars.

"I can't breathe."

"You're not expected to!"

Moustaches were shaved as the Church in Wales frowned on such protuberances. Clerical clobber was tried for size. Spirituality gave way to confusion. We all looked like stage parsons ready for a Brian Rix farce! Suddenly, there was no more time. We hoped that God knew what he was doing!

Ordination at Llandaff Cathedral has been reduced in my memory to a small black and white photograph of twelve deacons with shining faces and snow-white surplices, all standing in a row outside the Norman arch of what was to become the Royal Welch Regimental Chapel. Episcopal hands had been laid upon us.

"God help us!"

Life was never to be the same again.

My main thought was about D'rene. I had sat behind her in our Primary School in our home village, so we were able to share our childhood memories. Married in 1949, our first home was a flat in the Theological College and now all that lay ahead was "for richer for poorer; in sickness and in health ... according to God's holy ordinance".

We had no place to live as I had not been appointed to a Parish. I was a dog collar with no place to go. So we returned to our College flat in the old College buildings, which were still a shambles after failing a confrontation with one of Hitler's land-mines. There we waited for the ecclesiastical machinery to point us in the right direction.

No choice in those days was given to us deacons. We were directed to a parish. That was never questioned. The Warden of Ordinands was the man with the power to control our future. His name was Gwynno James and he had been my mentor for years. Before I went off to war, I had spent a year at Cardiff University. Gwynno had been the Warden of the Church Hostel, St. Teilo's Hall, in Roath. We had talked long and often into the small hours of the night. He was the first person I could question about the faith with all the doubts of youth. I had attended with him a conference for ordinands at Aberystwyth University, where for a week the Rev'd Dr. George McLeod of the Iona Community had led the sessions. It had been a great experience, although I had not realised at the time how important our lecturer was.

McLeod had been appalled at the Church's lack of commitment to the working classes at a time of high unemployment and poverty in West Scotland. In 1938, he founded his Iona Community and with a group of unemployed men he went to Iona to rebuild the monastic buildings of the Medieval Abbey. Lord McLeod of Fuinary completed the project in 1967.

Gwynno remained a vital influence in my life until his premature death in 1967, when he was the Dean of Brecon. That year he had asked that I conduct the Holy Week addresses in his Cathedral, but we did not know that he would die in the February. He was a great and good man.

In his book, 'Letters to John', Gwynno ended the first letter with these words: 'Our worship should be like a car; if it runs smoothly and easily, all is well, but if it starts and stops, something is wrong. We want to speak to God with a quiet ease, we should be relaxed and feel quite at home. No sudden jerks, no convulsive movements, no clamant voices, only a quiet movement towards God.' His life was a quiet movement towards God.

For my first appointment, I was asked to visit the Vicar of Glyntaff, near Pontypridd. This pleased me, as I had spent many a happy childhood holiday with my cousins in Pontypridd and I knew the area well. How could one forget creeping down the stairs in the middle of the night to listen to the wireless as Tommy Farr was only just beaten on points by the legendary Joe Louis! I had been born in the neighbouring village of Cilfynydd and, whilst no member of the family still lived there, I was happy to return to my roots.

It was raining, a typical South Wales drizzle, when the clouds sit wearily on the mountain rims, making the day grey and long. D'rene and I had set out from Llandaff by Western Welsh bus to view the promised land of Glyntaff. Arriving early for my appointment, we explored the Parish Church. It was dirty, dark and damp. Tattered Prayer Books were scattered about the pews.

"Funny smell." D'rene's nose was twitching.

"Stale incense."

"It could do with a good clean."

"Don't volunteer!"

The whole place smelt of dust and neglect. I left D'rene in the church (she had not been invited!) as I went to the vicarage to meet the Vicar on the dot of three. I was not happy!

Neither was that Vicar! He viewed me with suspicion. I stood on the doorstep in the drizzle. The sight of him in a woolly cardigan and tired slippers did not encourage me. He telephoned the Warden of Ordinands. It was a vague conversation at our end. Letters had obviously gone astray. He agreed that he needed a curate, but the parish had problems. He tried to explain it to me. The interview was apparently over.

I told him that my wife was waiting in the church. No tea was offered. Mention of D'rene and furniture seemed to upset him further. He thought that there might have been difficulty about the house, but if I had been appointed, there might be a possibility of digs, although that would not have included a wife! I was as puzzled and confused as he was.

I rescued D'rene and we fled Glyntaff, bewildered but relieved that it was a non-starter. Wet and tired, we found refuge in our flat back in the College at Llandaff.

Next day I called on the Warden of Ordinands. Gwynno was very angry.

"You are not going to Glyntaff!"

The implication was that neither would any other curate. I never did discover where the fault lay and decided that it was better forgotten.

A few days later, I met John Elwern Thomas, the Vicar of St. Fagan's, Aberdare. We sat on a park bench on the other side of Cardiff in Waterloo Gardens in Roath, at three in the afternoon. It was like a game of Russian spies and I hoped that I was being brought in out of the cold!

Amongst the roses it was all agreed. I did not even blink when he said there was no house, but he assured me that one would be found. I was to be licensed to serve in the Parish of St. Fagan at Trecynon with special responsibility for the District Church at Cwmdare. So with a promise of a place to live and a proposed stipend of five pounds a week, our future had been decided. It did not take very much to make us happy.

# 2.
# THE ARRIVAL

Bishop John Morgan was not big in stature, but he ruled his Diocese with a rod of iron worthy of Cyfartha Steel Works. He left no room for discussion. He decreed that D'rene and I were to remain in the College in our flat until a house was found in Trecynon. Meanwhile, he asked that I travel to the Parish every Saturday, reside at the Vicarage, perform my Sunday duties and return home to Llandaff on the Monday. I was to work the proverbial parson's one day week!

That edict did the trick. A house was quickly found, but needed to be put in order. At last, it looked as though I was about to start my ministry. It had been an untidy initiation; yet we were young and innocent and knew no better.

The top end of the Aberdare Valley is the loveliest of places. The town sits in a vast basin with the Parish Church of St. Elvan and its glorious spire at the centre. The Parish of St. Fagan was two miles to the north and was really just an overflow sprawl with no design or signs of planning. My particular patch, Cwmdare, could not be seen at all; it was a sort of ditch into the side of the hills. I was to love the place.

Aberdare is rightly called the Queen of the Valleys, the Crown being the surrounding mountains. Those crags and cliffs would guarantee that, whatever the direction of the wind, the clouds would be uplifted by the majestic heights, ensuring that a deposit of drizzle be vouchsafed every day. This was to be my kingdom.

Finally, with a new dog collar, a marriage of one year and a ten year old bike, I had arrived. That bike was almost the end of the beginning. The date was the back end of 1950.

The tiny hamlet of Cwmdare had been built to be ignored. No person would see it unless he had a good reason to call. It was full of Evans's, Thomas's, Jones's, Davies's and Williams's and one or two others. The approach was by the steepest of hills with the road disappearing over the brow into apparent nothingness. That was where Cwmdare began. Up on the top of the hill, the valley opens out again and stretches to its farthest corner under towering cliffs, tinged with a glory of heather and bracken. It was lovely in all its moods, even though at the far end lay the Bwllfa Colliery.

Cwmdare is surrounded by hills, to the south, west and north. The river is, of course, the Dare - hence the Valley of the Dare. The beautiful crags to the west are called Craig-y-Bwllfa and the Bwllfa colliery sat at the base.

This was Cwmdare. Our home in Trecynon was about two miles away at the bottom of the hill. Every visit to my little flock meant that the hill had to be climbed, day after day and in all weathers. You could not ignore the weather.

Surely the greatest discovery of man is not the wheel, but the plastic mac ... no Welshman would survive without it! We carried them, neatly folded, held together by elastic bands. We were recognised the world over and easily made friends, as we used the weather to open every conversation. If it wasn't raining, it was going to and, if it was, it was about to stop. The safest opener is ... "We're about to have some weather!" Wales is wet. From September wintering into April, we endured it, but never in silence. At least, our summers were superb, because we all enjoy warm rain. For me, on my arrival, the challenge was to be the combination of the wet and the hill ... and that bike.

The brakes on my bicycle were designed to be squeezed, ineffectually, against the rims of the wheels. They were meant to be adjusted by a child, but were beyond my intelligence, as I could not make the back blocks make contact with the back wheel. I should have persevered. The front brake was of moderate value in the dry. I remember, in colour, my first encounter with the wet!

At the bottom of the hill was Cemetery Road and, naturally, the cemetery. I charged down the steepening incline with the brake full on. Every sinew was straining, but I was gathering momentum as I went. The brim of my hat was bent up by the wind flow, as I literally hurtled towards the cemetery. Quick thinking saved me. Down I swept and, at the bottom, I made a sharp and skilful lunge to the left and shot up the road at an alarming rate out of the parish in the general direction of Hirwaun. Flying aeroplanes during the war had been safer.

Our new home was the Old School House in Trecynon, alongside the Parish Church of St. Fagan. The Infant and Junior Schools were in use and we were to occupy what must have been the Headmaster's domicile in the last century. It was very old.

When we arrived, we met the bucket brigade. The welcome was tremendous. The ladies from our church in Cwmdare had marched down the hill with buckets and mops and brushes and distemper. Each lady had a scarf, tied like a turban on her head to protect her curls and her curlers. They were a formidable bunch of females, who knew how to work and create much noise in the process.

This was the first time that I realised that there was a natural division between those up the hill and the softer folk down the hill around the Parish Church. No doubt was allowed about my allegiance. We were adopted on the spot with a warmth, which came easily to valley people, showing affection with a generous simplicity.

They came to clean and decorate our new home, but above all they made us feel welcomed. It was a good start.

We were surprised to discover that our three storied house, plus basement, was already occupied. The living room was damp and, in order to disguise it, a partition had been fixed to battens to cover the worst affected walls. Behind this partitioning lived a colony of lively mice. Every morning when the bucket brigade arrived, the first task was to remove the drowned mice out of the pails of distemper. Some were not quite dead and were released into the freedom of the school yard. A new breed of magnolia rodents could have been discovered in Upper Aberdare. The mice never went away. When we were sitting quietly in the evening, reading on either side of the coal fire, our friendly co-residents would emerge and join us in the comfort of the hearth. There they would sit on their hind legs, twiddling their whiskers. It was a happy compromise to accept each other and battle would not be rejoined until the next morning. I grew rather fond of mice.

There were other residents in the house, apart from us and the mice. I loved D'rene's apple tart and it was very fortunate that clear Pyrex glass plates had been invented. We were never to eat a tart, which had been kept on the cold slab in the pantry, without looking underneath. Too often, the bottom of the tart was black with ants. No food could be left uncovered in this pre-fridge era.

Yet we were always warm and comfortable. Our carpets ... they could only be bought if you purchased other furniture ... were laid on the flag-stoned floor. In spite of all our efforts, we failed to avoid the outline of the stones working through to mark the carpet. The damp completed their ultimate destruction. Perhaps, like everyone else, we should have stuck to linoleum and loose mats.

Long ago, Cwmdare became a dot on the map because coal had been discovered. With the people came the chapels and our church. The first church was a small building on the Bwllfa Road, which was followed in 1887 by the present yellow brick structure in Queen Street.

Some three hundred houses settled on the hill and spread themselves along the road into the valley which was called Cwmdare. At the far end sprawled the two winding towers of the pit and a muddle of sheds. Most of the houses were set in neat terraces with little or no front gardens, each row branching off the main road, like the bones of a fish. It was a tidy little place with squares of brightly coloured linoleum on each morning-stoned door-step. Everybody knew everybody. Even the cats and dogs were on nodding terms, in the daytime.

Three pubs served the thirst of the valley ... the Ton, the Colliers and the Castle. The dog collar was not expected to visit those establishments. The hunger of the valley was met by three fish and chip shops, open every day except Sunday. God was fully catered for in superior stone and brick. Notice boards were not needed. These were the places where God was called upon to meet His segregated congregations, dividing His attention without prejudice between Elim (1867), Nebo (1868), Gobaith (1875), the Mission (1911) ... best galvanised, of course ... and St. Luke's (1887). My job was to look after the last one and stay in it!

The pubs and the chippies and the churches were not in competition. We all knew where we belonged. The ground rules had been well defined by those who had gone before us. Part of my task was to read the body language, watch my feet and keep my bricks airborne. Above all, I had to get it right the first time or the word would go forth faster than any jungle drum. No training had prepared me for this.

The ecclesiastical pecking order was as set as the Athanasian Creed and equally incomprehensible. Discussion was neither expected nor encouraged.

"Good morning. I'm your new minister."

"We're chapel."

"Sorry about that."

You were checkmated by the first move of the game. Then would follow the intensive brain washing, worthy of the K.G.B. It was very subtle. Decades of their Free Church contacts were trotted out, often with references to their family Bible, to be followed by an eulogy on the sanctity of their present minister. At least, they usually got the name right and I quickly realised that they were talking about the place of worship which they would attend should the matter ever arise. I was not expected to pursue the subject any further. This allowed us to move on to the weather and, on that subject, there was no discord.

"Not a bad day."

"I've seen better."

"Could be worse."

"It'll clear up by evening."

There was no safer subject and quickly mastered.

No coal ever emerged from the Bwllfa Colliery ... only miners! The coal was being brought to the surface, but arrived on top in the neighbouring valley on the other side of the mountain. We never saw coal and no-one ever talked about it. After all, that other valley was like the other side of the moon and was as difficult to visit. So in Cwmdare we processed miners. These men entered the mine and returned at the end of their shifts at the Bwyllfa. We had no coal dust in our valley!

On the 1st January, 1947 the National Coal Board came into existence. The Bwyllfa Colliery had been closed in 1938 and the two hundred foot chimney stack was removed in 1944. This had seemed to be the end of the coal era for Cwmdare, but in 1949 plans were started to rejuvenate the Rhondda Fach in the next valley and also to re-open Cwmdare. An underground roadway (3,200 yards long) was driven from our Bwyllfa to the Maerdy pit in that next valley. That was why no coal was to appear in our little village. I arrived just as the new system swung into action.

The day shift was six to two, the afternoon was two to ten and the night was ten to six. Most miners stayed on the same shift week after week. Double-decker buses brought in clean men and then removed the dirty. In Cwmdare, we had three rush hours on the road, except on Sunday. My great discovery was that along with the men, as the big wheels wound up the cage, came the fleas.

Fleas loved me. The men came home from underground, still wearing their working clothes, heavy boots, trousers tied with string, dirty jacket, shirt, muffler, cap, bag on shoulder. It was like a scene from Richard Llewellyn's "How Green Was My Valley", without the singing. That film had not mentioned the fleas.

As a small boy, I had visited the stables at the Meiros Colliery in my home village of Llanharan in the Vale of Glamorgan. There the sick and tired horses were cared for in the clean air above the ground. Almost seventy years on, the remains of the pond and stables still are to be seen today, if you know where to look.

The pit ponies had long left the Bwlffa, but their fleas were pleased with my arrival in the valley. My contribution to the Cwmdare ecology system was to provide the blood.

At the end of my first afternoon, when I had taken my dog collar on exploratory house calls, all had apparently gone well and I had arrived safely back home, complete with bike and black hat.

Bishop John Morgan had issued an edict from his palace in Llandaff that all his clergy, at all times, were to wear a clerical hat to symbolise their office. We obeyed.

The hats came in differing forms. Cathedral Canons sported black rosettes on the front of their hat bands. Rectors tended to perambulate their vineyards under rice pudding basins. The rest of us did what we could. Mine was very large. I felt like a pale, washed out, Al Capone. All the younger clergy were convinced that the Bishop toured the Diocese, incognito, on hat spying missions. We all had second-hand stories of his Lordship's telephone calls to our vicars, when he accused us lesser mortals of being about the Lord's business improperly dressed. The twelve apostles would have had a rough time in our Diocese! So we kept our black head-gear screwed on, even on the hottest of days. But, at the end of my first afternoon's visiting, I had other things on my mind.

I never actually saw a flea, but the evidence was there on my nether back regions. A routine was quickly established. At the end of each afternoon, I removed my shoes and stood in the bath fully clothed. Slowly, I unpeeled myself, like skinning an onion, carefully examining each article of clothing. D'rene stood by to supervise and pounce on command. We both knew that they were there, but as my vest was finally removed, all that I wore was a puzzled look ... not a flea to be seen! There was only one conclusion. I was a carrier!

My task in the order of the universe was to scatter fleas about the parish by stealth. This meant that, wherever I went, I was to leave behind me a fellow traveller. I hoped that it would not be noticed. Daily I endured the bath routine, gathering goose pimples and further bites. We never found a single flea.

As the weeks passed, the problem went away. I could only assume that my blood proved to be inferior, with an alcoholic content of zero. Eventually, pit-head baths were installed and life-styles changed. The colliers still came home with caps and mufflers, but their faces shone with carbolic.

Having mastered the bike, the mice, the ants and the fleas, I was all 'set to go'. I just hoped that the good folk of Cwmdare were ready for me.

# 3.
# CONSOLIDATION

Visiting those houses was a joy. In my ignorance, in those early days, I thought that all that was required was to knock firmly on the front doors and wait. I tried it. Nothing happened. Wherever I went, the village seemed to be deserted, until at last I discovered how to make house calls, 'valley style'.

Those front doors were never locked and the way to effect entry was simple. I parked my bike, unlocked, against the front parlour window ledge before giving a firm ecclesiastical knock on the door and then pushed it open and shouted.

"Hello, Evans the Curate."

It never failed. There must have been at least two dozen Evans's families in Cwmdare. I was classified and, as far as I knew, acquired no other nickname.

"Come on through."

That meant along the passage, ignoring the front parlour door, by the staircase, into the middle room and at last down a step into the kitchen, which was the nerve centre of the home. Beyond the kitchen was the scullery and the back door to the outside privy and the coal house. That was the design of almost all the homes. The kitchen fire was lit, summer and winter, and was the only heat in all the house. We were tough in those days.

The front door steps not only carried their pieces of bright lino, but were daringly sporting brilliant red lino paint. This over-bright modern invention avoided the daily stoning of the step. You were expected not to tread on the paint. Later that red was to spread around the bricks of the doorway and then appeared on the front window sill and finally up the sides of the windows. Next the scullery floor was painted and the steps up the back garden. They were firmly into red lino paint.

The front room was called the parlour. There on the multi-coloured carpet was the best three piece suite with myriads of small cushions from Aberdare market and, in this supreme comfort, the family bicycles were safely housed. In the window space sat an aspidistra with the curtains, pattern on the outside, tucked around the plant. You could stand peeping through the vegetation at the big world of the street and not be observed. Spying was a refined art. Under the aspidistra was the large black family Bible. It was never read. In it were listed the births, marriages and deaths of each generation. Sadly, those lovely plants and the Bibles were eventually deposited into the dust bins, as we progressed into the age of the motor car and one-parent families, although I am told that the aspidistra is these days attempting a bit of a come-back, but not the Bible!

The middle room housed two wooden arm chairs, one either side of the fire-place, which was filled with dried flowers, gleaming brass fire-irons and the family copper kettle. Large mirrors dominated the mantelpiece, reflecting the array of sepia photographs. There the generations sat ... hair pulled into tight buns, ankle length gowns, men with waxed moustaches and hats in hand across the waistcoats. They all looked down in judgement. And that was where I was expected to sit on my first visit to every house. It was rather formal, but I was 'the cloth', respected but not accepted.

High tea was served at the four-chaired table with its hand embroidered cloth.

"Lovely cloth, Mrs James."

"Made by our Gwen. God bless her."

"She's not ..."

"Consumption. Only twelve when she was taken."

"Is there a photograph?"

My skills grew, but I need not have worried as the topics of conversation were clearly placed like visual aids and no frivolity was expected. If all went well, I would be pressed to bring Mrs Evans next time. The meal was always a marathon, as the table groaned and I dared not refuse a crumb. That ordeal over, all following visits took me straight through to the back kitchen.

"Evans, the Curate."

"Come on through, bach!"

That was when I knew that I had been accepted.

The front parlour remained a mystery, until I took my first funeral. That was where the coffin was placed for all the villagers to pay their last respects. The widow would remove the lace-edged handkerchief off the face of her husband and without fail each caller would remark on how well he looked.

"There's lovely and peaceful he looks, Mrs Griffiths."

Then the undertaker would make the last call.

"Anyone else before I screw him down?"

I was never fully at ease with that routine. Then the coffin was balanced out through the front window into the hearse.

When all was done and the men had returned from the ceremony an hour later, the high tea was produced as by magic. Ladies in full wrap-around pinafores moved in with plates of food, all good neighbours. The men drank whisky in the parlour. The Curate was given one glass, regardless of protest. Actually most of the men never drank the stuff ... but it was a funeral! The women controlled the middle room where the table creaked under the ham tea. The closer neighbours supervised the kitchen and cared for the widow as she sat by the fire. In turns, we popped in just to 'have a word'. For some strange reason, it was always the men who were called to meet their Maker, whilst the women just grew older.

The hub of the house was, without doubt, the kitchen with its wooden chairs and chenille tablecloth. The fire was never out and the mantelpiece was resplendent with two white china dogs amidst a fine collection of brass candlesticks. There were never any candles. The kettle remained on the hob and next morning's sticks were in the oven in case they were needed.

I never actually saw any dusting, brass polishing, mat shaking or dish washing. The kitchen looked lived-in, warm and welcoming. It was always spotless.

"Sit you down. The kettle has almost boiled."

Tea was ever ready. Coffee was never mentioned, although most homes owned a bottle of Camp ... all chicory and water. As far as we knew, in our ignorance, Brazil produced nuts and not coffee!

The women would sit at the kitchen table, chatting the news out of each other, whilst, to my astonishment, there before the fire was the man of the house sitting in a tin bath. No-one seemed to notice. In front of me in the middle of the afternoon, the day shift was scrubbing down, warmed by the four-bar coal fire with its twin hobs, two ovens and simmering kettle.

Then there would be the bubbling boiler full of potato peelings for the pig in the back yard and a large iron pot with food for the men. Those stews gathered strength for days. And, of course, there was always the bacon with rich fat for fried bread and a good crispy rind, browned and curled in those pre-cholesterol days. The houses breathed the smell of food.

There in his tin-tub was the man of the house. No words were needed, but it was obvious that Mam was proud of Dad. His back was never washed and, as a result, it shone like ebony. Apparently his strength was not to be weakened by water and the logic of that statement was not to be questioned.

Life-style changed with the arrival of the pithead baths in 1952. Then cars began to fill the streets and the bicycle slowly disappeared. Next came television. It was the end of conversation in the valley.

No longer would the family sit around the table to enjoy the food and listen to their elders.

"Children are to be seen and not heard!"

"Sit up straight and eat your greens!"

"Out to play now!"

There was obviously a topic not for tender ears. 'Divorce' was a word to be whispered. A 'single parent' was a positive scandal. We could never have guessed what lay ahead!

In the midst of all the friendliness, I was not allowed to be one of them. That was no surprise. My Dad had been the village policeman - Evans 410 in the old Glamorgan Force - and we children were the offspring of Evans the Police. I saw many photographs of my father in rugby kit with his waxed moustache, but I suspect that even in the scrum, he was a man apart. A quarter of a century later, I never revealed in that mining community that my Dad had been a Bobby and that he had been actually involved in the infamous 1926 strike, when Churchill had called in the troops. The valleys never forgot and never forgave. The fact that my father had been struck by a brick and had remained unconscious for a number of days would have evoked no sympathy and no understanding. Some things you must just accept.

The Curate was kept in his place, the people deciding where that was to be. Once for an experiment, and only once, I called in the Ton for a drink ... people forget that you can drink lemonade in a pub! Silence fell and quickly I was ushered into the back room and then the conversation was resumed. I was an intruder. Yet, when we went on our many coach trips to the seaside with the Sunday School or the Senior Guild, we happily stopped off at the numerous watering holes and I was accepted as good company. Here was another lesson to learn. The Ton was where the working men could meet and I had no part in all that. After all, they did need a private place to wash away the coal dust, whilst indulging themselves in their problems and difficulties. Never again did I attempt a 'social call' in the Ton or the Colliers or the Castle.

The War was only five years past, but apart from food rationing, which was still with us in the early Fifties, there appeared to be little interest in those world shattering events. Quickly I realised that no-one wanted to know about my years flying aeroplanes in the Royal Air Force and there was even less thought about my adventures overseas. Life was contained not just in the valley, but in the village and even within the street. This was hard to believe.

Very early during our years in Cwmdare, D'rene and I found a wonderful friendship with one of the Church Wardens, who was known to all as Auntie Esther. Her husband was a retired miner, called Tom. Esther played a major role in my Sunday marathon.

Up the hill to Cwmdare, I pushed my bicycle for the 8 a.m. Communion Service, which was followed by bacon and eggs at Auntie Esther's. Her favourite encouragement was, "Eat a belly full!" I did. At 11 a.m., we all returned for the Children's Church, which I had started. It was a winner. Over one hundred children attended in all weathers and each Service was an organised riot. There was to be no better training ground for the art of communication, as each youngster had an attention span of about fifteen seconds. We sang, we leapt about, we performed plays and, in the process, became a family thoroughly enjoying worship. I am certain that there is laughter in Heaven, apart from the odd bit of silence and the twang of a harp.

On the bike, I swept down the hill for lunch to return sharply back up for Sunday School at 2 p.m. The children appeared in droves, together with a band of teachers headed by Auntie Esther. I took a group of the older boys, aged fifteen and sixteen, and we huddled together in the small vestry. On their seventeenth birthday, they were pensioned off! Never again was I to have contact with young lads of that age and today it could not happen. When the afternoon was lazily hot and the gnats were flying, we sang a hymn and marched up Queen Street to a grassy spot called the Patches, each class selecting a hollow. We had a quarter of an hour, by my watch, for the lesson of the day and then we scattered the sheep, as the rest of the time was a romp of games and laughter. I hope that those children, who are now well into their fifties, remember those care-free years of not long ago.

Back down the hill again I sped for tea and a break with just enough time for D'rene and me to walk back up for Evensong at 6 p.m. The Church was invariably full. Under my nose, alongside my prayer desk, were three rows of youngsters, who had attended the morning and afternoon sessions. That was not the end of it.

When Evensong was done, we all had a stretch and a walk, as we chatted to each other for about ten minutes before we resumed our seats for Singing School. New hymns and chants for psalms, solos, duets, trios and quartets, all helped to rattle the rafters for another hour. At last we knelt for the Vesper Hymn and the Blessing. Most stood in the street and chatted happily before turning for home and their coal fires. It had been a proper Sunday!

Supper was served at Auntie Esther's with a post mortem on the day and no punches pulled.

"Very good, Evans." That was Will.

"I'm off!" That was George, off to the Ton.

"Many there?" That was Tom, who never went.

"Bit more Bible, Evans!" That was Esther.

"That smells good." That was me.

It was a perfect way to learn my trade.

Supper had been in the oven for hours. It was invariably a repeat of the Sunday lunch, meat, gravy and all the trimmings. Then would follow apple or gooseberry tart with large helpings of warm, thick custard. Never before had I eaten such food, sufficient to keep us alive for the week! It took all the pain out of rationing and we did not ask any embarrassing questions.

I was convinced by this time that, in the valleys, as soon as you knocked on a front door, there was a mysterious arrangement, which pushed the hob with its kettle across the fire. One phrase was common to all households. After greeting each other, out it came.

"I'll just go and open a tin."

Before you could reply, there was a tin of pears or peaches or mixed, and there the lady of the house would stand, clutching her large loaf of bread to her equally abundant bosom, carving energetically slice after slice of the thinnest of rounds.

It was that hill which kept me thin!

# 4.
# HIDDEN TALENT

In those early months, I kept hearing odd references to a 'little book'. In the end I foolishly fell for it and asked the question.

"What's a little book?"

They had been dropping not too subtle hints that it was time to produce an operetta. This was unveiled to me during an open forum at the Sunday Night Singing School. Democracy is dangerous! It was decided that we tackle Snow White and the Seven Dwarfs. Actually they told me that this was the one for us, so it was not much of a discussion.

As by magic, a complete script with words and music was handed to me on the spot and we promptly ordered one hundred and fifty copies. It was an act of faith, not covered by text books or ever mentioned in the job description at College. Obviously I was meant to learn quickly how to produce an operetta. Apparently I was in charge, regardless of previous experience, which happened to be nil.

It was Autumn, Harvest Festival was over, and we were firmly into 'show business', whether I liked it or not. The thought did occur to me that I would be known as Evans Snow White, but I knew that it would be a hard-earned title. At least, it would be better than Evans Ali Baba!

The chorus work was sung with gusto each Sunday evening after the service with Dai Cul (Culverhouse was the name of his abode and was used because his correct surname of Morgan only added confusion in a valley full of Dai Morgans) on the organ and Edwin Mear, the Shoemaker, was in charge of the baton. I presumed that as Edwin spent his days with a hammer in his hand, he would find the baton a natural tool. The organ was an old fashioned harmonium with foot pedals to pump (too much enthusiasm and it tended to rock in rhythm with the feet), at least three non-working stops and an ongoing wheeze.

I sat back in amazement. Whether part of the cast or not, we all sang until we were word perfect and could whistle the tunes in our sleep. I soon realised that every person present, men, women and children, intended to be on stage and in the chorus line. This was going to be powerful stuff and I just hoped that the stage would bear the accumulated weight. Our chorus girls were well built, not a principal boy amongst them. The spin off for me was a full church every Sunday night. Snow White had the edge on Cranmer.

The back-room preparation was under way. We booked the Miners' Welfare Hall in Cwmdare for the Dress Rehearsal on the Easter Monday and the Aberdare Coliseum, which held eight hundred people, for the rest of the week. We had fixed our dates and the pressure was on.

After Christmas, rehearsals began midweek in the Welfare Hall. D'rene set about the costumes for over one hundred children because, apart from the seven dwarfs, we were blessed with troupes of elves and fairies in assorted sizes. Allowance had to be made for chip consumption between Christmas and Easter. Stage and off-stage tasks were delegated. There was no problem about co-operation; everyone wanted in on the act.

Principal singers had to be found. A young lady with a superb voice, previous experience on stage and the necessary measurements, was persuaded to play Snow White. She was a winner. Auntie Esther's sister, Doris, had a rich contralto voice and made rather a superior Wicked Queen. Our Dan Walters, one of the sidesmen, played Idle Jack. The dwarfs were selected with care and a prayer. Tickets had to be organised for the five nights. Every member of the cast paid a subscription for the privilege of attending each rehearsal, including each child! No-one missed a session lest the place in the pecking order was lost, so we had all the monies for the production. I was surrounded by enthusiasm. Nancy Lace came to the rescue, so that we could introduce more movement on the crowded stage and the final touches were added by Lesley Vivian, a school teacher friend. Lent passed rather quickly that year and was almost unnoticed in the growing excitement.

There was no way in which this production could fail. Each cast member came from a large family, scattered far and wide. Some even attended rehearsals ... six pence on the plate, please ... to urge us on to greatness and to keep their protégés on the ball.

The week of the show became a blur of frenzy. I lost my voice, which must have pleased the cast and contributed to the eventual success. Doctor Simpson offered me sympathy and tablets, but even he seemed more interested in the progress of the Show than in my well-being.

Each performance in the Coliseum was started with the audience standing, so that we might say a prayer together. My husky voice was interpreted as emotion. On reflection, that now seems a strange way for the evening to open, but even the cast behind the closed curtain joined in the prayer. At that time, this was right and proper and was naturally received. Nothing went wrong.

The high spot for me was when Mansel Morgan, aged five, dressed as a cherubic elf, clumsily tripped backwards over a toadstool and slowly somersaulted up stage to land smiling on his feet. The audience roared approval at such acrobatics, whilst his mother threatened to murder him. Every stage-hand belted out the choruses and I swear that some of the audience were joining in to produce a volume of sound worthy of a choir of five hundred. This was good stuff, typical Welsh treble forte rendering. My voice was not missed.

An unforgettable moment came in the final chorus on the final night. The back row of chorus girls was packed with ladies on the wrong side of fifty, who lay on their heels and bellowed the immortal words, 'O, Happy Day! O, Happy Day!' This was the final wedding tableau with all one hundred and fifty on stage. The sound echoed around the Coliseum into an ever-increasing crescendo just as Doris Williams, centred in the back row, fell over into an epileptic fit. I crawled behind to drag her off as the climax reached the final bars. It was done.

The Sunday after Easter is called Low Sunday because the congregations are normally very slim. St. Luke's was full that night. We were packed to the door, as we applauded each other. Of course, it was an anti-climax; so we all agreed that we would put on an extra show that following week in the Welfare Hall, just for the fun of it and for the families to take a relaxed look at their stars.

That week the whole of Cwmdare held its breath for the Thursday edition of the Aberdare Leader. The press did not fail us. Countless copies were sold and sent around the world. With editorial guile, every member was mentioned by name. Even Evans the Curate was granted a couple of lines and I was never to forget them. After singing my praises the eulogy ended '... obviously the Rev. Evans is a good producer of children.' There was not to be a 'little book' again, but in good time D'rene did produce three lovely children. Well done, everybody!

# 5.
# HARD WORK

Life settled into a pattern almost immediately. There were surprises. I soon discovered that any attempt to visit all the people in Cwmdare was doomed to failure. Most parishioners expect the clergy to call with a regular beat because after all, "He's got nothing better to do!" That was also my opinion at the start. A house visit takes more than half an hour to be of any value. Sadly the days were too short. This left me with a sense of failure before I had barely begun.

About this time I heard a story which every parson should take to heart.

"I hear we've got a new vicar."

"Yes, but he's not much good."

"What's the matter with him?"

"He's got foot and mouth disease."

"What's that?"

"He can't visit and he can't preach!"

I felt that I was a prime candidate for the disease.

The work was harder and more exacting than I had envisaged; knocking at doors and getting to know the congregation was a superhuman task. The chronic sick were seen on a monthly visit and each one took the expected half an hour as we shared communion ... there had been a previous call just to set up the formal occasion. In time these sick folk had to be seen weekly and, at the end, I made a daily call. The more people I contacted in my rounds, the more there was to do as time spiralled away. I struggled to find time to relax.

My first Christmas was a blur of activity. In most homes there was the smell of puddings, cooked in cloths in the back kitchen boiler. That ritual was to disappear as in later years we resorted to ready made varieties in coloured boxes. Today the children no longer stir the pudding mixture, making a wish as the shining six-penny pieces were dropped into the large bowl. The wish was that they would reappear on your plate on Christmas Day! No-one at that time was able, or expected, to take a week off and disappear by plane to the Costa Lotta in the sun. We sang our carols in our churches and chapels, but we, of course, were convinced that we were the best in St. Luke's.

In College, we had been assured that we would not forget the first funeral. That was true; the scar remains today. There I was, all set to go for it. The body was in the front parlour, last respects had been paid and the cover was safely fully screwed down. The undertaker clutched his top hat to his breast and gave me a conspiratorial nod. I was neatly sandwiched in the corridor of the home between the middle room and the kitchen. The congregation filled the house and stretched into the street. All eyes turned to me.

With courage, I struck up "Aberystwyth" and was immediately surrounded by glorious harmony. Hitting that correct note had troubled me for nights, but after that I thought it would be plain sailing. I read from the Bible and followed with a prayer or two. That was when it all went wrong and I was praying that the floor would open up.

"Let us say the prayer Our Lord taught us."

This was my cue for the congregation to join in with me. Off I started with "Our Father ...". There was silence about me. No problem, I thought, and promptly forgot the words! There was complete silence.

"Say it in Welsh, boy."

This was a stage whisper from the undertaker at my side. Undoubtedly that was sound advice, except for the minor detail that my Welsh was minimal. Happily I recalled the opening phrase and in a good loud voice chanted out, "Ein Tad." The valley sighed with relief and the prayer was taken up by all. It had been a close thing. Later in the parlour I was told, "That was a nice touch to leave the English alone. Well done, boy." I hoped that no-one had noted the long moment of panic.

My confidence grew sufficiently to invite the other local ministers to most funerals. They in turn did the same to me and we travelled together, a solemn posse of prayer. The word "ecumenism" had not been voiced abroad, but we knew instinctively that a death in the village was a grief to be shared by all.

We opened our lungs and eased back on our heels at Harvest time. In honour of St. Pumpkin we 'ploughed the fields and scattered.' We closed our churches to tour each others' tabernacles. Sermons were long, full of scripture and the sins of the flesh, never had there been such thumping of pulpits and competitive purple passages. We gazed with smugness on each other's Harvest decorations and to outdo them all, we in St. Luke's lit every candle we could find. Visiting clerics were called to read the Bible and lead us in impromptu prayer ... many must have thought that their watches had stopped! Harvest done, it was time for Winter.

Next came the Singing Festivals, at which we attempted to outblast each other to the Glory of God. We in St. Luke's were hot on anthems to be sung by the whole congregation. All music was taught by tonic sol-fa in our childhood and it enabled us to tackle most compositions. Dai Cul pumped hard on the rocking harmonium, until it almost burst its bellows. Edwin, the Shoemaker, swung his baton in an effort to outface the Last Trump. These were the days to remember! Little did we realise that they were the "last days", because change was around the corner. Television, the motorcar, the money to burn, the end of the family, all this was waiting in the wings. Time was running out and the valleys were to sing no more. Who could ever believe that by the end of the century there would be no coal-mining in Wales!

The Miners' Welfare Hall was the social centre for the village. It held the all important billiard tables, not that Evans the Curate was allowed to acknowledge their existence. I knew my place in the order of things.

As a child, I was never permitted to visit the local billiard hall in my home village of Llanharan. That hall had the grand title of The Arcadia. To this day, I have no idea what produced such antipathy in my parents and in their parents before them. We children tried peeping around the front door of The Arcadia, but the inner doors were always shut and there was never any sound. All the windows were boarded up. I knew that it was full of men in caps, which never left their heads, and that each man kept a Woodbine screwed into his mouth. They all looked happy to me and, whilst billiards must have been in some way evil, it was obvious to us kids that the side effect was good.

Every Monday afternoon I called at the Miners' Welfare Hall at 3 p.m. on the dot. There I met Nick. He was the master of ceremonies for our Monday Whist Drive. Everyone attended. At 3 sharp, tea was served in real bone china cups and saucers with a fairy cake on the plate. Evans the Curate was always given two cakes and I visited every table. The cards were not on view! Twenty minutes later, I departed and the game continued. The Chapels held their Whist Drives on the other afternoons with almost the same participants, but I was not invited. Incidentally, the Non-Conformist ministers never visited because, I assumed, card playing was officially the work of the devil. Auntie Esther was a regular at the tables and was able to keep me abreast of the latest news ... at least, that which was suitable for my tender ears. I suspected that Esther in this way was to direct my house visits, but the system worked to our mutual advantage, as a clergyman was supposed to know where to visit without being asked!

People like 'doing something'. Quickly I discovered that I only had to 'ask or suggest' for action to follow with ample volunteers. My task was to 'have an idea', shout for help and, above all, be prepared to roll up my sleeves.

A small group of the men agreed with me that the paths around the Church had seen better days, having been reduced to pot-holes and puddles. One Saturday we mixed concrete and completed the job, which to my certain knowledge has now lasted for well over forty-five years. Each of us stuck a nail into the concrete by the vestry door ... I wonder if they are still there!

This activity got us thinking and the brave decision was that we were to erect our own Church Hall. All that I asked was that we did it at the speed of the giving. No-one liked borrowing money. "If you cannot afford it, don't buy it!"

The site at the back of the church was on a major slope. For weeks, we built a superb retaining wall, using the stones we plundered from the mountain side. Two hectic days were then spent filling a lorry with spoil from one of the coal tips and in-filling for the foundation. I had to admit defeat; there was no way in which I could keep up with those miners. My contribution to the whole project was to complete the foundation. Work was then to pause and it was my successor who eventually acquired enough cash to purchase the pre-fabricated hall. To my knowledge it still stands today.

Fish and chips were vital to survival in the valley. We boasted three establishments ... the Bwllfa, Queen Street and Dare Road. This guaranteed that the aroma was everywhere. Each family had its own chippie. I quickly grasped the routine. One house visit said it all.

The men were home from the day shift, the bath tub had been returned to hang on its nail by the back door and the coal fire was in full heat. At the table sat the men. The table was covered by a brown chenille drape with bobbles at its edge and, on that, was a white, lace-bordered cloth, hand made and starch stiff. There in the centre was placed a very large meat dish and on it, straight out of the oven and still wrapped in yesterday's Western Mail, were enough fish and chips to feed the Pontypool front row. Each man, in total silence, ate his way into the centre, until the last crispy bits had disappeared. Those chips were delicious and I can still smell them. Then the men would fall back into their chairs for a snooze, before the evening stroll to the Ton. Then there would be conversation. The curate and the church played no part in this way of life, although both were treated with the utmost respect, as long as we kept our places. I was learning my trade.

So the days were to stretch into weeks. Ahead was an examination to pass before I was made priest. I read some books, which I barely understood and on one occasion pointed this out to my tutor. I was told not to be surprised and accepted his advice to get to grips with the parish work and not over-worry about the examination. It was good thinking, as most of the studies seemed irrelevant to my little flock in Cwmdare. The main task of the parson appeared to be knocking at doors and listening to people. There was no need to say very much.

When eventually I was ordained priest in St. Dyfrig's in Cardiff after a week's retreat at the college in Lampeter, no-one in the parish thought that much had happened, except that I was then able to celebrate Communion on my own. My vicar, John Elwern Thomas, had briefed me well. He led by example ... what other way is there? This opened up a fuller life and at last I felt that I was doing the job which I understood

... and that it was the job for me.

The brief we receive on priesting is concise "... visit the sick and bereaved and preach the Gospel." The doing of just that became my life's work. There were to be many tangents and temptations, but I believe that at the end I was able to keep that brief to the letter.

# 6.
# THE THREE OF US

School House was to become a home. D'rene soon came to terms with the mice and the fleas, the steep stairs and the high ceilings and the shortage of money. There was never a penny to spare and D'rene had to keep careful accounts. Then came the inspiration. I was young and naive, not knowing that inspirations could be fatal, start wars, end marriages, bring down governments; they should be kept in firm control. Thanks to my particular flash, I was convinced that we had discovered a way to produce extra income.

It was the advert in the Aberdare Times which was responsible for the brain-storm. The facts were there before us, in black and white.

'Grow your own mushrooms and make a fortune.'

The truth was not to be doubted, because there in print were the names and photographs of the smiling ones who had achieved their ambitions and, thus encouraged, we promptly sent off five pounds to purchase the mushroom spawn. That was one week's wage! It had been saved over many months for D'rene's winter coat.

Happily, we had a large and rather damp cellar. Expertise was to be no problem because the enclosed leaflet was lucidly clear and I followed the instructions to the letter. I carried endless buckets of soil from the Vicarage garden, down the steep cellar steps, in order to create the mushroom bed. The Vicar was puzzled, but co-operative. In those days, many shop's wares came wrapped in straw; so I acquired a sack and did the rounds. Everyone was inquisitive, interested and full of

"Let us know how it goes" comments.

The straw had to be cut into half inch lengths. Down below in the cellar, we laboured with a garden shears, in all the dust, by the gloom of a single light bulb. Next came the gallons of water as we mixed the soil and the straw. At last, all was ready. The theory was that, left for a set period, the bed would produce the necessary heat. The spawn was sown. The light was dimmed. We waited.

Right on time, the little white dots appeared ... and then, promptly disappeared! Actually, we were to pick one mushroom, which had cost blood, sweat, tears and a fiver. Inspiration and perspiration had not worked. I wearily carried all the soil up to our flag-stoned backyard and there we created an instant flower garden. That summer we grew wonderful blooms, but sadly could not eat them. The experience left us not overfond of basidiomycetous fungi!

D'rene had not been feeling too well and eventually took to her bed with glandular fever. Doctor Simpson cared for the folks at the top end of Aberdare. He was a good and wise man, both respected and feared. He was known to stride up the stairs, take one look at the patient and re-appear in the kitchen with his instructions.

"The patient needs a wash now. Put clean sheets on the bed. I'll be back in half an hour."

No-one ever argued with Doctor Simpson. His word was law. A bowl of water and a clean towel were placed on the wash stand, which graced every bedroom. The water was in a large flowered jug and it sat in its matching flowered basin. If there were problems, the neighbours would come to the rescue, as the doctor's progress had been under full observation. Windows were opened for the first time that century and fresh air enjoyed every corner of the hastily dusted bedroom. At last, the good doctor returned. His quick appraisal on the initial visit had told him that all that was probably needed was good nursing and the odd bottle of coloured medicinal compound. Most patients recovered from boredom and a surfeit of female nursing. Illness was far more simple in those days. A visit by the doctor was a last resort as he was 'not to be bothered'. Death was "a blessing".

We all loved that doctor, as he stood head high over most of us, exuding a calm which I suspected was no more than a pose to cover the inadequacy of his chosen art. His authority assured us that any known disease would be quickly sorted. In a miraculous way, everyone felt better after his visit.

D'rene stopped Doctor Simpson in his tracks. He was making a return call, the back door was never locked and the front door was never used. I was out and about doing my parsonical bit. Up the steep stairs the good Doctor climbed, calling out his name. There he found D'rene. He twinkled as he told me the tale later.

She sat, propped up by the pillows, with a shoe-last between her legs, a hammer in her hand thumping away at a sticky rubber sole, which she was affixing on to a pair of my shoes. Shoes in those days had to wear for as long as possible. His opening words were a statement. "Well, D'rene, you must be feeling better!"

The window-sill in our bedroom was very high and only by standing on the bed could we look out on the street. One night we were tucked up rather early, as can happen to young people, when we heard a dog creating, Baskerville style, out on the road. We leapt on to the bed and on tip toe peeped out of the window. It was worth the effort.

Opposite us was a terrace of two up and two down and straight across lived a character called Dai Price. Dai never spoke to anyone and I doubt whether he actually noticed anyone, but, if he did, all they received was a grunt. I believe that Dai had given up on the human race and, at his age, felt that he was entitled to drop out.

That night there he stood, under the lamp post, in his night shirt. His thin white legs shone like match sticks, as they disappeared into his old lace-up boots. whilst in his hand was a black, iron saucepan, out of which he was carefully emptying haddock water into the gutter. A neighbourhood dog was doing his bit to control the environment and Dai, still with his boots on, was balancing on one leg and aiming at the dog with the other. Dylan Thomas would have enjoyed our street.

A few days later, I was called out by the neighbours. Smoke was pouring out of Dai Price's house. I was not sure whether I had been summoned to bless the conflagration or to put it out. They had timidly knocked on Dai's front door, not too hard lest one of them had to confront him. As there had been no response, they feared the worst, and in their minds it was a job for the parson.

"Get the police."

This was my reaction, especially as the Station was only fifty yards away down the street, but I suspected that the good folk had not wished to disturb the local constabulary. Policemen must be handled with care and as seldom as possible. We had very considerate neighbours.

Jones, the Police, arrived, parked his bike at the curb outside Dai's, removed his cycle clips and attracted a larger crowd. This was becoming an event. They stood gazing with approval, as the law and the church discussed the matter.

"Is Dai in?"

"There's no answer."

"He must be out."

"What about the smoke?"

"Probably a fire."

The conversation had been entirely logical. There was no way around the back, because the gate was high and covered with barbed wire. I became decisive.

"Let's break in."

I thought that this was a positive suggestion. Jones went a little pale, but used his initiative.

"Try your boot, Evans."

He favoured delegation. One kick did it. The passage was full of smoke as we worked our way through to the kitchen. Three bolts fastened the back door and, once it was opened, the smoke began to clear.

I have never forgotten that house. One side of the entry passage was stacked shoulder high with chopped wood, neatly piled. Each corner of the living room was packed with similar sticks, lined up like soldiers on parade. In the kitchen the smoke was pouring out of the oven, where Dai was drying yet more sticks for the next morning's fire. Dai was not up stairs in either of the two bedrooms, but we discovered that, even up there, the walls were stacked high with newspapers.

At last, Dai came down the road from an excursion to the wet fish shop and caught the curate and the policeman emerging from his home. He did not express any surprise and was not in the least disturbed at our 'breaking and entering'. On reflection, we should have known that he would be calm, as he always had a smoked haddock look about him and we, at last, knew the reason why. Smoking sticks to him meant that they were dry and ready to be stacked. The parting shot of Jones, the Police, made his position quite clear.

"Better find someone to fix the door, Evans."

I did it myself under Dai's supervision. Thereafter Dai seemed prepared to acknowledge me as a friend and at least, in his mind, he had discovered a use for the clergy.

About that time, we came across the joys of Canasta and it almost turned night into day. Halfway up that hill lived the Vivian family, Gwyn and Huw. Their daughter, Lesley, was a teacher in our Church School, which on Sunday doubled as the local Welsh Church. Lesley was a regular popper-in for tea and a chat at the end of the school day. They were a happy family and we laughed a lot. I had visited grandmother Sproule at their home, as she had set about her departure from this world. That old lady taught me much about caring for the terminally ill. There had been precious few guidelines at College. Above all, I learned that conversation can be full of tangents and not one was to be ignored.

Towards the end of her time, I would sit at Gran Sproule's bedside talking about the olden days, which all the elderly can recall with twenty-twenty vision, even though they cannot remember whether they had eaten breakfast that day. There was one occasion when out of the blue, she fixed me with one eye and cut across the conversation.

"You did not say 'Good morning' to the Bishop".

That stopped me in my tracks with not a thought left in my head. There was nothing to say.

"Do it now."

I must have looked somewhat perplexed.

One eye seemed to be all that she needed as she kept the other firmly shut. I did ask her once about that closed eye and all that I got was that she was resting it. I believe that she was just winking at her departing world with all its oddities and absurdities. The Good Lord had given her a superior sense of humour.

"Go on," she said. "He's on top of the wardrobe."

So I smiled and bade the bishop a "Good morning!". That seemed to satisfy her and the conversation tottered on. She was probably pulling my leg and enjoying herself at my expense, yet it might have been reality, as folk at death's door seem to move into a world where the past, the present and the future are merged. Is that what is meant by eternity? She died surrounded by love and I still remember her with a smile. She was a lovely lady.

At the end of the day, often late in the evening, D'rene and I visited the Vivian's bungalow to play Canasta. As the coal fire disappeared into ash, we moved the card table nearer to it and almost sat in the hearth. Blankets around our shoulders, we continued to play. One game could last six hours! Years later, I discovered that we had misunderstood the scoring system. The result was that we crept down the hill in the small hours and when, months later, Stephen was born, he accompanied us on our Canasta marathons. We hoped that the pram wheels needed no oiling, lest we would have alerted our neighbours to ready gossip.

At that time, there was no need for a Neighbourhood Watch Scheme, as it was as natural as breathing. Back at School House we would enter quietly, not even putting on lights. So we crept to bed. It never worked. Lace curtains are infallible. By mid-day the next morning, the Vicar had been fully informed of our nocturnal antics. It took time, but we found the mole!

It was a lady who lived just across from us, endowed with the most remarkable antennae, never missing a single move in the street. She apparently did not need sleep. The Vicar, John Elwern Thomas, was waylaid with ease and given the information with nods and winks. However, he was totally indifferent to such gossip and we had a good laugh together. All that mattered was that I appeared bright eyed in Church at 7 a.m. every morning. That must have been when our mole went to sleep.

A new curate was to join the staff. He was to be responsible for Llwydcoed on the other side of the parish. It was regarded by 'our lot' as the posh part, where people had front and back lawns and the men wore white shirts on weekdays. We in Cwmdare thought little of them. I cannot recall ever being asked to preach in their church, even though we were in the same parish! With all Christian charity, we hoped that the new man would be happy in Llwydcoed ... and stay there. Valleys are narrow places.

The ecclesiastical grapevine told us that our new man, Harry, was not too good in the mornings. The Vicar suggested that we both set a good example. God must have a sense of humour. It had to happen.

That first morning after Harry had joined the staff, he and I sat in our clergy stalls and waited. In the end, we started Matins on our own and in the middle of the second lesson in marched the Vicar, muttering something about cheap alarm clocks. Time was not mentioned again.

For a young, inexperienced curate, the request to conduct the Three Hour Devotional Service in the hallowed Parish Church was flattering. I accepted with pleasure. Today, with grey hairs, I would hesitate.

There are many excellent books with advice on the Good Friday Three Hours and I started my preparation at the beginning of Lent. Hymns and Psalms were chosen. I wove my addresses around the traditional Seven Words, which our Lord spoke from the Cross. Everything was written fully in my note book, each section timed by the clock. My preparation was as masterly as all the books advised. Nothing was to be left to chance. There was not a better primed parson in the Diocese.

In fairness to me, it had not all been plain sailing. D'rene had been taken into Abernant Maternity Hospital on the Thursday before Holy Week and our first born had arrived on the Saturday. Incidentally, all three of our children were born on a Saturday, which chanced to be my day off. D'rene's younger sister, Edna, came to stay over that Easter weekend and was mainly remembered for using chocolate essence in place of gravy browning. The taste was not too bad, but was not to be repeated.

As a proud and tired father, I faced the matter of Good Friday. At one minute to noon I climbed the pulpit steps. I knew that the congregation would 'come and go' during the singing of the hymns and naturally hoped that many would stay to relish my eloquence. Such is the humility of youth.

My composure wobbled as I gazed down at the sparse numbers. Right bang in the middle of the front pew sat Vicar Hughes. Canon Hughes had been the previous Vicar of the Parish. He was old, rigid and stern, a legend in his own lifetime and truly 'canonised' in the folk memory of Aberdare. His eyes never wavered for the full interminable three hours of my torture. The screw was being turned.

Timing was vital. Three hours go on for ever. To my consternation, I began to run ahead of schedule and I realised that I would run dry well before the end. Some wit said that the guillotine concentrates the mind. I had to improvise. The congregation can only take so much silence, so I was left with the only safety net available for the parson. We call it extempore prayer. It was a long three hours, but I had survived. Arrogance had long departed.

As D'rene was still in hospital with Stephen, I was invited back to the Vicarage for the inevitable fish pie. There also was Vicar Hughes. I waited for the verdict. Here was the man who had terrorised curates and had dominated everyone in the valley for three decades. Part of the legend was that he had made most of his house calls in the small hours of the night, always leaving his card. 'The Vicar called and received no answer.' At last he spoke. 'Thank you for the prayers, Evans.'

That was it. No mention of the hours of preparation, which had produced the script. All that was ignored. Much later I realised the wisdom of his comment. The only natural content of my whole effort had been the improvised prayers and it must have shown. I learned that lesson well and, thereafter, discovered how to speak from short notes with just enough written to keep the theme in sight. You cannot read to communicate from the pulpit and if you cannot hold your thoughts in your own head, you will never transfer them into any other.

D'rene and Stephen arrived home after ten days in hospital and life was never the same again. Here was a new topic of conversation wherever I went. D'rene became remarkably fit, as we pushed the pram up the hill and hung on to it as we returned. Advice poured over us and the ladies clucked their admiration. Easter eggs arrived by the ton and were duly devoured by Mum and Dad. My sermons were coloured by thoughts of new life, a ready Easter theme. Half crown pieces were pressed into Stephen's hand and a Post Office account was opened. People were kind. The Baptism followed quickly. Life in School House had changed. We were three.

Out of the blue came a letter from the Bishop of Llandaff. John Morgan was a bachelor and it was obvious that his work was his family. We were that family.

When I was an ordinand, he once took another friend, Frank Jenkins, and myself to St. David's Cathedral, as he was officiating at a Confirmation Service there and we had a wonderful time together.

During the war, he had written regularly to me, as to all his ordinands.

Every time that we were on leave, we called at his home in Llandaff; he had set aside a Tuesday morning for his ordinands to 'pop in' without appointments. There the Bishop would sit at the hearth and serve coffee from thermos flasks. He became a true 'Father in God'.

His letter on the birth of Stephen was welcomed by D'rene and me. He spoke of Simeon in his old age, feeling that all was well as he knew that the Christ Child had been born and that he could die in peace. 'Now lettest Thou Thy servant depart in peace ...' The birth of a son, he said, was all that parents could pray for and we should be happy. We knew what he meant. Children are the future.

# 7.
# THE FAMILY

The parson for the first year of his ministry is called a Deacon. This is indicated by wearing his stole diagonally across his chest and, of course, by the newness of his cassock and surplice and the aura of untried innocence. A year is long enough to sort out all that, as the corners are rubbed off at the expense of the poor parishioners. After priesting, the stole hangs vertically and, at last, the man is allowed to celebrate Communion, take marriages and bless all about him. It is not an easy time. I was lucky. Auntie Esther with her husband, Tom, and the two adopted sons, Will and George, had provided me with the base camp for that testing first year in a dog collar.

Sunday night at Esther's was for us the high spot in the week. One evening was exceptional. D'rene and I had thoroughly enjoyed ourselves. Neighbours had popped heads around the door, tales had been coloured, the walls had bulged with laughter as the reminiscences grew in the telling. We set off for home with light steps. All was well in the world.

That was the night that Auntie Esther's Tom in the small hours quietly came down the stairs, disturbing no-one in the household. The next morning, Esther found him hanging in the kitchen. Tom was dead. We could not believe that the tragedy had happened.

We searched our consciences. There had to be a reason. Tom had been so normal that Sunday evening, full of tease and fun. With his slight stammer you could never guess what he would say next. Now it was over.

In a while, we realised that Tom had been deeply disturbed, knowing that he was suffering from serious hardening of the arteries; he had rationalised the implications as unacceptable. His little knowledge of medicine had proved to be dangerous. Sadly, he had not shared with the family his fears for the future. The contrast to this mental state was that wonderful last evening we had shared together. In the midst of the fun and laughter, Tom had already bought the rope that he was to use in his suicide. Even today, I find it difficult to understand.

*We all loved Auntie Esther.*

I have discussed Tom's death with many people and find one inescapable conclusion. We may think that we understand the person in front of us; the truth is that we have no idea of the inner suffering and even less concept of what actually goes on in the other person's mind. We must then take this thought further. We are not in the position to offer free advice to anyone; as we can never be absolutely certain that we are hearing the complete truth. Also, we can hardly be in a position to pass judgement as most of us barely understand ourselves.

It was many years later that the Bishop of Liverpool, Clifford Martin, on the eve of his retirement, expressed the same thought to me.

"I hope in my forty-five years in the ministry that I have never given any advice to anyone, but I pray that I was given the wisdom to ask the questions, which they were afraid to ask of themselves."

Little did I know that my time in Cwmdare was coming to an end. Now as I look back over the last fifty years, D'rene and I still count as our dearest friend that nonagenarian known affectionately as Auntie Esther. Many years after Tom's death, she married Will, the young lad whom they had adopted. She was after all only four years older than he was. They had adopted four children originally, three boys and a girl, all from one family. One boy had died and the girl was eventually taken by another family. Esther had been only twenty-one when she took on this ready made family, not knowing that there would be no children by her own marriage. Tom and Esther were full of love and shared it with us. Today she is blind and lives in a Residential Home.

This is the lady, who in her grief allowed her love to shine through and showed us all how to live and deal with sorrow. Such folk are rare.

I was to remain in Cwmdare for only two and a half years and knew that there was much more to learn about my calling. At least in that valley I had discovered how to visit people in their homes. I had watched folk die quietly with dignity and felt the helplessness of only being able to hold their hands. Many times they had asked me to pray, which I found almost an embarrassment and an intrusion on their privacy. This surprised me as I had expected it to be a natural activity of the parson. The truth was that God seemed to be doing quite well without my stammering interference at such an important time. I even suspected that the dying were trying to make it easier for us who were left behind. People attributed powers to me that I did not recognise. All that I knew was that I was inadequate, yet I was invariably thanked for the strength that I apparently gave. This remains a mystery to me. I shall never quite understand the remarkable power which flows from the simple emotion of love. Love is better expressed with a squeeze of the hand than a wealth of words. Maybe that is all that we can offer to each other. Dying is a full-time occupation and we parsons should not get in the way with over-pious words and platitudes. I was learning.

Another discovery was that the work of the parson is not all sweetness and light and that there were those who seemed to take a delight in denigrating anything which I was trying to achieve. Some were plain rude.

The rudest of all were the strange characters who boasted that they were blunt and honest and proud of it. My earthly reaction to them was a heaven-sent desire to punch them on the nose, although I must admit that I might have been mistaken about the origin of such a lovely thought. Obviously there are foolish folk whose 'honesty and bluntness' causes endless pain to their families and to those who had to put up with them. Quickly I learned that I was not alone in attempting to understand these insufferable, so-perfect characters. We all endured their pride and, in time, I almost felt sorry for their blindness to all the fun that was passing them by in life. I suspect that my smile must have maddened them, especially as I went overboard to thank them for indicating my such obvious shortcomings.

Turning the other cheek adds a new dimension to life. It works! No-one has any idea how to respond. Later, I was to discover that it was useful to point out to the person who complained about me that, not only were they probably right, but that the situation was far worse than they had discerned and, of course, I was ever grateful for their perception, as they were well placed to help me with my problems. Most would find themselves involved and assisting to their great surprise. In the end, I accepted that the complainant at least had shown an interest and should not be ignored.

Our lives are moulded by people; some we copy subconsciously, others by their example show us the way not to go, but we are fortunate if we meet the person who at an early age can give direction to our existence. Such a man for me was Gwynno James.

My first encounter with Gwynno was when I applied for a Welsh Church Scholarship before going up to Cardiff University. The vital interview was in Cathedral Road in a large imposing Victorian building, which housed the Representative Body of the Church in Wales ... that title was off-putting! A group of us candidates sat in the ante-room awaiting the confrontation. Gwynno stuck his head around the door. Round faced, cherubic, bald and dog-collared, he beamed at us through gold wired glasses.

"Don't worry, lads. Give all your answers to the chairman. If you don't know the answer, say so!"

It did not help! The interview room was large enough to hold a dozen or so grim faced clergy with the chairman at the far end and one empty chair. I cannot recall how we arrived at the subject of my School Debating Society, but I do remember my reply to the question.

"I've never won a debate yet. I'm always asked to speak on the wrong side."

"We know the problem."

That was the chairman. All must have gone well because I was awarded a Scholarship ... and was to meet Gwynno James many times.

Growing up in the small village of Llanharan in South Wales, I discovered many characters, all of whom have had an influence on my character. Mary the Back always stood at her doorway with folded arms over a wrap-around pinafore and she never missed a jot of a move in the village. Tommy Tossle wore a beret with a pompon on top. Just the once I called him Mr.Tossle and received a clip about the head for my trouble. Later, mother explained that his name was Tommy Williams ... I never did quite understand what that was all about. In Wales, all the Evans and Williams and Thomas tribes have to be given identification. Billy Go Deeper was a coal miner with only one piece of advice. Phipps the High Corner kept the pub on the village Square. There were Jones the Station Master, Morgan the Chips, Dai Hop the Grocer, Coffin Williams, Lewis Stocks and Shares ... the list went on. Mrs. Long John was over six feet tall and from Pembroke; she was not Welsh!

Although we were a 'church' family, I was sent to the Welsh Chapel on Monday evenings to pick up a bit of the language. It was called Band of Hope. As ever, we all sat in circles and read the New Testament in Welsh. That was the first part of the evening and was entirely incomprehensible. The second session was even more of a mystery. We sang endless choruses and were told about the demon drink. At the age of six, I signed the pledge and had been totally brain-washed against alcohol. I had, of course, never touched the demon, but along with all the other converts thought it sounded just the stuff for us. Children never understand adults.

Choruses were regarded as too non-conformist and not to be sung in our Church; we tackled the psalms. But in that Welsh Chapel we young ones belted our best out of every chorus we were taught. Especially we liked 'Jesus wants me for a sunbeam' and to a man we ended the refrain with the totally irreverent but satisfying words '... and a bloody fine sunbeam am I.' Bopa Sara, who was in charge of us scallywags, had a purity of mind beyond our grasp. Another favourite was the hymn, Bread of Heaven, which we duly mangled. Our final translation was at treble forte.

'Bread from Richardsons,
Cheese from Hopkinses,
Beer from the Turberville.'

One evening, I arrived home ostensibly from Band of Hope, having spent my penny collection on sweets, to find Bopa Sara sitting in our kitchen inquiring after my health. I had not arrived at Band of Hope! So once again, it was bed with no food and, to my delight, I was not allowed to go to Band of Hope after that. That was supposed to be a punishment. Adults are very odd.

Our bungalow was on the village square, opposite the High Corner pub and the address actually was "The Bungalow, The Square"! This was a great vantage point. I was much impressed, as a child, to have a grand-stand view of a drunken punch-up, which was settled when P.C. Baverstock strolled down the Council Hill, grabbed each contestant by the collar and smacked their heads together. Today he would have been dismissed from the Force and probably imprisoned for assault! Without a word spoken, he resumed his gentle walk. Justice is better seen to be done. Now that I could understand.

Just the once Jimmy Thomas and I tried to drop stones down the funnel of a passing train. The engine had stopped at the platform of the station a mile further on to inform Jones, the Station Master, and on receipt of this information the local Bobbies made a classic pincer movement. Jimmy and I were marched off to the Police Station. One of the Bobbies was my Dad. Pushed into a cell, we awaited our fate. Mrs. Thomas arrived and administered instant retribution. Eventually I was taken home, my evil way of life was discussed and, yet again, it was bed with no food. Happily my brother Frank was courting Zena, and, as we lived in a bungalow, the window was edged up and chips from Morgan's the Chip-Shop came to my rescue. Zena and Frank were a good source of fodder, although I suspected that it also ensured my silence whenever I came across 'goings on'. Silence is golden, but only when rewarded.

Another character was Johnny Pinkott. He was actually called Johnny Pinkott, because there was no way in which even the Welsh could add to it. Johnny had religion in a big way, but was suspect because he was neither Church nor Chapel. He was a free thinking evangelical with the gall to mention God on other days apart from Sunday and this he did with legs apart, arms up in the air, in the street and in a loud voice. All denominations frowned upon him, as he caused discomfort with all his chat about God. This was used as proof that Johnny was not quite with us. It was the simplest explanation of his apparent nodding acquaintance with the Almighty.

One day, I met Johnny Pinkott head-on in the Square, outside Bert Beard's the Blacksmith. There was no escape. He stood bandy legged, armed with a walking stick, baggy black trousers, no tie and a battered hat.

"I believe you are going into the Church, boy."

This was a powerful opening broadside for a fifteen year old with little to say and even that with a stammer. My silence was not noticed, as he went in for the killer punch.

"Has God spoken to you?"

My dumbness was complete, which was just as well, as Johnny was not indulging in a discursion.

"God spoke to me in Porthcawl."

He waved his arm in the vague direction of that seaside resort.

"I was standing on the promenade, watching the sea, and placed my hands on the railings. They were vibrating with power and that was when God spoke to me."

Suddenly, he seemed to expect me to speak.

I had nothing to say. Johnny turned and left me with no further explanation, heading for Reg Smith the Butcher, his stick acting like a rudder as his legs shot out sideways with minds of their own. I worried. I, too, had stood on the promenade at Porthcawl, as the sea crashed magnificently over the top and all that I had done was lick icecream. God must have been very selective to pick on Johnny.

At no time for me had there been any flashing lights, no crash of thunder, not even a small still voice. I just knew that I wanted to be a parson and had made that quite clear to the family at an early age. The local incumbents in turn, Vicar Jones and Vicar Corney, had led me through the early years as a choir boy and then an altar server. Vicar Corney had briefed me at the age of fifteen, before I travelled to Llandaff to meet the forbidding Bishop John Morgan. My Vicar stressed one point to remember.

"Don't mention music because the Bishop is an expert."

All advice is good when you are going into the unknown, armed with the ignorance and the arrogance of youth. That interview remains etched into the archives of my mind.

The Bishop's Palace at Llandaff was large and I felt very small as I entered the open door, clutching my Bridgend Grammar School cap for protection. There was no need to be nervous. The Bishop was great.

A large dog had sniffed me as I went into the Palace and, then, in the hall the Bishop threw a ball down the passage. Off the hound went, putting on his brakes half way along to end up in a heap at the far wall. I was promptly dispatched to the opposite end and eventually finished with the ball in my hand and the dog on top with its legs pinning me against the wall. Then we sat on the floor, in front of the study fire, to enjoy tea and cream cakes. I had forgotten that it was called 'an interview'. The Bishop chatted away, popping in the occasional question. One stopped me in my tracks.

"Do you knit?"

My astonishment must have shown. He went on to explain that men were often the best designers, the top chefs and the finest painters. The word 'chauvinism' was not in common use in those days, but I suspect that the Bishop would have replied that he was only stating the obvious. I nodded as wisely as I could.

"Do you like music?"

There it was, the trap question, and I fell for it, lulled by cakes and dogs and episcopal guile.

"Yes, I love music."

"What do you make of Bela Bartok?"

For all that I knew it was a skin disease. I had never heard of the name!

"I love the psalms."

The Bishop beamed and went across to his grand piano. We sang. I still had the remnants of a treble voice and together we delighted in the 23rd and the 150th. Here was a man who understood that in Llanharan the only available music was to be found in the Church choir, and that was what we discussed.

We talked of David John Kinsey, our choir master, who made the boys feel his tummy as he breathed in deeply and, in turn, showed us how to fill our lungs. We chatted about Miss Jones, who treadled her way on the swaying harmonium, holding on to the bottom note long after we had run out of puff. Bishop John Morgan accepted me as an ordinand and some ten years later he was to ordain me.

Gwynno James remained the Warden of Ordinands for many years and was able to keep me in sight as time passed. During my first year at Cardiff University, I stayed in St.Teilo's Hall, a Church Hostel in the Parish of Roath. Gwynno was in charge.

That year in St. Teilo's, before I disappeared into the Royal Air Force, was invaluable. To Gwynno I was able to pose all the questions which youth thinks are original and shattering. At that age I misunderstood the Adam and Eve stories, questioned the existence of God and could not accept the resurrection's apparent absurdities. With Gwynno I had no hesitation in voicing my doubts and ignorance. He spoke well and I was able to understand. The more we talked, the more there was to doubt and, in this way, I made the simple discovery that a faith, which cannot stand up to questioning, will not be of any value. In this way a theological foundation was laid at a pace I could accept. At a time when most young people of my generation gave up, because there was no-one to talk with, resulting in the dismissal of God through almost total ignorance, I was establishing a faith which has travelled with me ever since. Ignorance and a closed mind make happy bed-fellows and result in darkness. It was Gwynno who sorted me out for the years ahead and my involvement with war.

Towards the end of 1952, a letter arrived from Gwynno James, asking me to leave the curacy in Cwmdare and suggesting that I join him in the mighty Parish of Roath in Cardiff. When I returned from the Forces at the end of the war, I had again resided at St. Teilo's Hall, which was then being run by the monks of the Community of the Resurrection. This meant that I had already lived in the Parish of Roath, St. Margaret's, for three years. The request to return was like being asked to come home. That I would accept was never in doubt. It was only in hindsight that I came to realise that Cwmdare had been not just my first parish, but it marked the end of a way of life which was fast disappearing from the valleys of South Wales. I had been fortunate to be there.

Cardiff was twenty-five miles from Aberdare and we had no money to spare. A date was arranged for me to visit Gwynno in order to discuss the move to the promised land and there was no alternative of getting there apart from my bicycle! I could not afford the bus fare and expenses were non-existent at that time. At least, it was downhill all the way. The return journey was not to be thought about.

It was a meeting of old friends and I knew that all was well. There appeared to be no problems. I was to be in charge of the district of Tremorfa with its Church of St. Philip. However, there was one slight small difficulty over the house in Tremorfa. It was not finished! A new three bed-roomed house was being built alongside the church and would be completed in the late Spring. As a holding operation, we were to be accommodated in a one bed-roomed flat on Partridge Road, off Newport Road. This was almost three miles from my area, but it was flat ... no more hills!

The farewell from Cwmdare was sad, as we had established some very good friendships; a few would last the whole of my ministry ... Auntie Esther, Les and Gwyn West and Mary Smart ... which is one of the joys of being a 'dog collar'. At that time, I did not know how rare it was in life to hold friendships for over fifty years.

We arrived in that flat with our houseful of furniture. The place was very small and we literally had to climb over our trappings to get into bed. The bath was in a sort of outhouse and, as the roof sloped, there was no way in which I was able to stand up in it. Naturally, the new home took a few months longer than had been envisaged to be completed. Through it all, D'rene battled with the conditions and Baby Stephen and with me and my bike. It was an unsatisfactory start to a new ministry, as I spent more time travelling than working.

Around Easter in 1953, we finally moved to Tremorfa, which actually made it the fourth house upheaval in four years and spoke wonders for D'rene's ability to organise curtains and create a home, but it was not that simple.

The moment that we opened the front door of the new house, we knew that all was not well. We could hear the drip of water. The kitchen floor was awash, as the stuff poured through the ceiling from the bathroom above. We sent for the builder. The removal men did their best. At last a man arrived. In the bathroom, he cut through the floor boards to locate the leaking pipe. We could hardly believe what happened next. He actually managed to sever a gas pipe! No water, no gas, no heat, as the rain continued to fall outside! No-one from the parish called to see how we were doing. We really could have done with the Cwmdare bucket brigade and the mice and the ants.

As that day wore on, the problems were sorted and we began to unpack. Fortunately Stephen was no trouble, accepting turmoil as his natural state. Then D'rene's parents arrived and the whole move fell into perspective. When they caught the bus that evening for the railway station, we knew that we had won. At last, I felt that we lived in Tremorfa.

# 8.
# SHOCK TREATMENT

Tremorfa is not a place.  On the map it is an area squeezed around the
remnants of Cardiff Airport, alongside the Rumney River and the
Dowlais Steel Works.  There was a beach of sorts at the far side of the
old disused airfield, but it was not much more than river mud, polluted
by the spent ore dumped on the fore-shore.  This ore, cooled into twists,
was inhabited by rats.  As the Steel Works dumped at night, the whole
sky smiled briefly with our local aurora borealis.  We ignored it.  A
fine orange dust descended upon Tremorfa when the wind wafted from
the west, and the wind was ever from the west.  The daily wash was
allowed one hour before the clothes began to change colour.  Some
five thousand people lived there in streets of look-alike Council houses
and we three were part of it.

Along the road were the shops ... a green-grocer, a general store, the
post office, a butcher, a chippy and a chemist.  Next along came the
Church hall and St. Philip's, which was endowed with galvanised
sheeting in washed out green, tired wooden once-white windows, and
standing guard at the front was a not quite upright, out-of-date, notice
board ... with no news.  Then came our new house, surrounded by
blackberry bushes, builder's rubble and a decade or so of used fish and
chip papers.  This was the social centre of Tremorfa and we lived in the
middle of it.

The population had been dropped there, after the First World War,
to escape from the tired streets of Splott and down-town Cardiff.  In

the nineteen twenties, it must have been a dream estate.

Most folk had only moved a mile or so from their original family homes with the result that the majority of those who were church-goers had kept their allegiance to their former parish churches and that was the way it had remained. They continued to worship in their 'home' churches. Our task in St. Philip's was to do our best with what was left. My new vicar, Gwynno, had been honest enough when he told me at my interview that it was a job for five years. The inference was that it would be long enough for any man. He was to be proved right.

Very quickly, I learned that in this place a clergyman was not made welcome. Cwmdare had been open doors and put the kettle on. Tremorfa was different.

Each house had a front garden with uncut grass and straying privet hedges. The whole place looked tired and neglected as the houses still showed the lack of paint and materials, the result of war-time austerity. My naive expectations were about to receive the shock treatment. The first time that it actually happened, I thought that it was just bad luck when, still wearing the statutory black hat and a clerical grin, I knocked at the door.

"Good morning. I'm the new curate."

"Bugger off!"

This was a new response, and in time I discovered that there were variants on the theme. The most common of them was, naturally, "Hold on ... I'll get the wife!" Soon I hardened myself, like any other door-to-door salesman, and accepted that any remark was the start of communication. It was better than silence!

At least, I understood. The reason was obvious. Here was a population, three generations removed from church-going, and they had no ecclesiastical or any other roots in Tremorfa. The way in which the houses were built meant that they could not even stand on their front door steps and chat to their neighbours as the gardens, back and front, completed their isolation from each other. They could not see any reason for the Church in any form and therefore the clergyman was an obvious parasite. Apathy was a way of life. I knew that no job was easy, but I also knew that there was no escape for me. Today the modern clergy indulge themselves in every possible sociological tangent, removing the dog collar at every opportunity. My job was to be a caring parson, get on with it ... and smile.

D'rene found it very difficult. Whilst they were able to dismiss me, the parson's wife presented an even bigger dilemma. D'rene had not been prepared for the treatment.

A visit to a shop was an education. As she walked through the door, all conversation would stop and invariably she was urged to come forward, in order to be served first. This she did as silence surrounded her. Obviously they did not know what to say, as though she was from another planet. Life in Tremorfa was not going to be very happy for D'rene and the final test was the pressure it inevitably put upon the marriage. We both knew that it was to be a battle for survival.

My major problem was that I really was not sure how to start. There was little advice available, as each parson had to find his own way with the gifts which were peculiar to himself. Such gifts were rather thin on the ground. Each parson felt isolated in his own pastoral patch.

The only hope for inspiration, which the Parish offered, was that every Monday morning at ten thirty the parish staff assembled with the Vicar at Roath Vicarage.

We arrived by bicycles from the corners of the largest parish in Cardiff. Roath was divided into areas with individual church buildings and clergymen. The main Parish Church of St. Margaret was surrounded by up-market houses, a world apart from my little vineyard. At St. Margaret's, the Vicar and a curate presided over the large and rather superior congregation, which paid no heed to the rest of us. Of course, in the same way the other four congregations in the daughter Churches did not wish to know that lot from St. Margaret's and this was because they felt that they were the poor relations. Actually we were the poor relations!

That hour on Mondays was all that was shared. There were five curates ... Owain from the Parish Church, Mike from St. Edwards, John from St. Ann's, David from St. Agnes's and me from St. Philip's. Theology played no part in our discussions. The meeting was involved in the art of delegation and the guile of raising monies.

Delegation was entirely caught up in poaching time from the men in the scattered areas, in order to provide help in the Parish Church. The movement was always one way and was not open to question. For me, this entailed a cycle ride at six thirty in the morning to take the early

Communion, a round trip of four miles. I silently hoped that God appreciated my efforts. Riding back home at 8.30 a.m., I breathed in the sickly odour of the Co-op Biscuit Factory and thought about breakfast. The spirit was in fine fettle, the flesh weak!

Money was concerned with the contributions both we and the Parish Church had to hand over to the Diocese for the annual and ever-increasing quota. This cash just disappeared into oblivion, as far as I was concerned. It never seemed to provide financial help for the parts of the Parish which were in real need of support, as we battled in the outer darkness of our wildernesses. Too often, I felt that it was an exercise in how a Parish should not be organised, but we were part of a time-honoured system. 'As it was in the beginning, is now and ever shall be.' The Vicar was caught in the same trap.

We young clergy were backed by militant wives, supporting each other as best we could and establishing friendships, some of which have lasted a lifetime. After the official staff meeting, we invariably held a second session over coffee in the eave-top flat of Bernard and Val. Most grouses were given a good airing and laughed into perspective. It was important not to take ourselves too seriously. Laughter is the best safety valve and the grumbling did no harm.

Just before my first Christmas in the Parish of Roath, St. Margaret, I attended a Parochial Church Council Meeting, which has remained etched in my memory, although I suspect that the event was never truly minuted.

When we were appointed, all the junior staff had been told that there would be a fifteen pound Christmas bonus. At that memorable P.C.C. Meeting, we assistant clergy, all five of us, sat together in the back row. Our expected role was to observe, learn and remain silent. That was the normal pattern, long established, but this meeting was to be different. John, who was the senior curate (soon to be replaced by Bernard at St. Ann's) to our astonishment leapt to his feet to make a point of order. The very act impressed us!

John had done his sums. We curates had been underpaid in the year by the unsurprising amount of fifteen pounds.

"Mr. Chairman, a point of order, if I may."

All heads turned to the back row. The Vicar seemed puzzled.

"Yes, John."

John's point of order was simple. How could the P.C.C. vote as a bonus that which was already ours by right? He popped this little gem just after one of the Wardens had put the proposal and before the other could second it. John had not consulted us, but to a man we applauded. The P.C.C. was silent. At last, the Vicar suggested that the matter be left in his hands and the business hurried along.

The next day we were all summoned to the Vicarage. Gwynno assured us that he had been unaware of the method of payment and apologised. So we all got our genuine bonus that year. Justice had been done, but little was achieved in our respect for ecclesiastical authority, which should have been above such malpractice. Yet through all the difficulties we experienced in that parish, not one of us felt anything but total respect for Gwynno. He was a wonderful person to work with and an example to us all. I believe that he was as bewildered by the peculiarities of stipendiary addition as we were. Fifteen pounds was a tremendous amount of money at that time.

There was only one place to start the work in Tremorfa. The small dedicated band of regular church-goers deserved my first priority and, as a result, absorbed most of my time. They were quite demanding and expected regular visits, even though I was to meet them every Sunday in Church. I could have settled into a comfortable routine and they would all have been well pleased. I drank their tea and complimented them on their sense of vocation, as I grew to know them better and understand their background. The truth was that the Church could not have continued without their dedication and co-operation. They deserved a pat on the back. I gave them just that, but began to feel that I was trapped.

The congregation was not interested in evangelism, although I doubt if that would have been admitted. In all my time in Tremorfa, I never met a Free Church minister or a Roman Catholic priest and it was clear that the vast majority of the parishioners were not in touch with any church and, unless I tried, that was the way it would remain. At least I felt that I knew the questions, even though there were no ready answers. There had to be a way. The main question was how to make contact with the community.

# 9.
# THE WAY IN

There had to be a way to visit a family, which had no connection with the church and had no expectation from the dog collar, without it proving to be an ego trip on my part or an attempt to create pew fodder. All that I could offer was the Church and all that it stands for; this could be seen as the centre of my activity and that activity was considered by most people to be just a 'one day a week affair'. In this way, the parson was rationalised out of the rest of the week.

To tell a stranger that you had called at his home to talk about God would seem to be the honest open approach for the parson, but it would have been met with incredulity and rejection. In my heart, I felt that all that I could offer was friendship, a genuine desire to get to know them and, in my language, to show them love in a hostile world. Even today, I am still convinced that this is correct and really is a starting point of all human contact ... just a simple "How are you?" and a quiet listening to the answer.

So I walked the streets of Tremorfa, knocked at doors, kept my inane grin firmly fixed and allowed my skin to grow thicker, as the rejection continued. I kept going, even though I had no idea as to what it was that I was attempting. There appeared to be no other alternative. God had other plans for me.

Every Monday, a group of pensioners filled the Church Hall. They were a self-contained group with no Church connection. By two in the afternoon the Hall was full and there was little Mrs Boyce banging away on the wreck of our piano, balancing precariously on her two cushions and torturing out the Old Music Hall ditties. Most of them sang. Then, they listened in all states of repose to speakers on any subject, as long as they did not hog the whole afternoon. Most were slightly deaf, but were there to enjoy the squash of companionship. Obviously, the vital ingredient for the afternoons was the time spent chatting over a cup of tea and a biscuit. If you lived alone or were lonely in your family, there was no better place to talk with friends. Tea was served at three on the dot. Many a speaker was cut off in full flow by the rattle of cups and the crash of trays. Here was an opportunity, which evolved naturally out of my desire just to be helpful.

Most Mondays, just before three, I would pop into the Hall kitchen, ostensibly to check that all was well with the equipment, then I picked up a tray and proceeded to distribute the teas. No-one questioned or objected to my presence. It was a point of contact and only took up half an hour of my time. At least, they began to know my face and my name.

Eventually I was asked to speak, just to fill in because the booked speaker had sent an apology. I was not sure what they expected, or even dreaded, from the earnest young curate and tea-boy. I read pieces from Three Men in a Boat and introduced them to H.E. Bates's Uncle Silas stories. I was asked again to perform at short notice, when they had no speaker or were let down. I became the hole filler. Eventually, with tongue in cheek and fearing the worst, I read some of my own stories of life in the mining valleys. These seemed to strike a chord, as many of them had originated from the hills and vales of South Wales. We were able to talk about old memories and share our nostalgia for the valleys. This pattern continued during all my time at Tremorfa.

The final proof of acceptance came when, to my utter surprise, they asked that I become their President. I was pleased and told them so when I was installed. My speech went very well ... I thought. I referred to the Chairman (she was Madam Chairman in those days) as the Queen of Splott. It was meant as a merry jibe and a compliment and was uproariously received. Much later, I was told that the Queen of Splott was the title they reserved for the local prostitute. At least I had proved that I did not know that!

A fair number of those good folk were to return to their Church, which they had abandoned as irrelevant some years before and that gave me much pleasure, but, above all, I was at last being stopped in the street for a chat as an old friend. We had matters in common to share. Without trying, I had discovered a way into one part of the community.

For the young people of Tremorfa, there was little else but the corner of the street and that was not very exciting, as no-one passed by after dark. The place was deserted.

I had little knowledge of Scouting, but felt that it might bring a different dimension into the lives of some of the youngsters, without thrusting religion at them. I assumed that ignorance would be no deterrent and that I would find support from the older element in the congregation. I was wrong. Happily, however, there was one man prepared to give some thought to the venture and he knew his stuff. He was married and had little time to spare, but he eventually promised one hour every Wednesday evening. It was enough for me.

The cubs met for the first hour and a half, then came the scouts for two hours. My expert helper gave half an hour of intensive instruction to each organisation, which was enough for us to form the Tremorfa Group. Our good friend wore no uniform and looked for no acknowledgement; yet his contribution worked like a charm. For a reason beyond my comprehension, the District Scout Commissioner insisted that I became the Group Scout Master and so, almost as an act of faith, we formed the 112th Cardiff Group.

I was delighted when the ladies of the Sunday School, led by Rita Johnson, adopted the cubs and proved themselves to be superb at creative chaos. Immediately, with the scouts, we had a waiting list and were able to form three patrols. Patrol leaders were selected and I met with them separately to digest the Baden-Powell Manual. I was to remain one page ahead. There was no lack of enthusiasm. We were in the Scouting business.

Money was scarce, but lack of it was merely an incentive to get it right first time and spend wisely. No financial help was available, apart from our own meagre Church funds. I believed that if you really wanted something, you must go for it. We all sported red and blue neckerchiefs and I was aware that I looked faintly ridiculous in my regulation length shorts. Ignorance must have been bliss, because the

Group never faltered, as we went from strength to strength.

Saturday mornings, we assembled with frying pans and billy cans and water bottles. Then we ambled our way to our glorious fore-shore, which was the rather sordid edge of the Bristol Channel, black mud, oily water and a positive nautical stench. Sausages were cremated and declared to be superb. Tea and cocoa were brewed, both tasting smoky and the same. We sang scouting ditties. Nameless knots were tied and unravelled and sometimes were correct. We practised until we had them right according to the book. Our faces shone with pleasure and grime. At the end of each Saturday morning, we even smelled like scouts.

After we had acquired some expertise, the inevitable request was made and I could not ignore it.

"What about a summer camp?"

"All of us?"

"We'll cope."

"I'll tell you next week."

I called a meeting of the parents and, as I expected, they grasped with alacrity the thought of their little darlings away for a blissful week. My Saturday morning adventures had given them a taste for peace. We talked ourselves into it and all eyes turned on me.

I did my homework. We possessed no camping gear, but I discovered that, if we went to the official camp site at Miskin in the Vale of Glamorgan, we would be able to hire tents and all the other items that were needed for survival. I made the booking. The hiring rates were low, but well beyond our means. The challenge would be to produce the cash in time.

The patrols went into competition with each other. Yet more Jumble Sales were needed. Not one of them doubted that we could do it. In those days, very few people went away on holiday and I was aware that this week, if we survived it, would be the high spot in these young lads' lives. Of course, we could do it! I swear that was when I began to go grey.

The date was fixed. I realised that there would be no help, just me and twenty-eight enthusiastic lads, all pretending to be scouts. This was a form of madness!

D'rene, as ever, was helpful and carefully worked out a week's menu of inter-changeable spuds, sausages and beans. For my own comfort, I had booked a small single 'Pup tent' with ground sheet and for the troop three large ridge tents. We convinced ourselves that we had covered all the necessary details. We were ready.

A couple of local tradesmen drove us, illegally, in the back of their vans into which we bundled ourselves and our bits of food and things. It was a fifteen mile bumpy journey into the country.

Poured out onto the site, we stood helplessly amidst the assorted kit we had hired from the equipment store. We had never touched a tent in our lives, but it looked simple! The time had come for me to exercise my expertise and initiative. After all, I was the Group Scout Master ... I knew this because D'rene had painted G.S.M. on my little enamel mug!

"The last patrol to erect their tent cooks the meal. The first to finish can light the fire."

The hours passed in happy chaos. My lads were delighted and totally committed. In time, our camp site looked almost Baden-Powellish.

We were not alone on the site. We had afforded super entertainment for the other well-ordered, smug, efficient, immaculate scouts who, at a reasonable distance, were our neighbours. They were wise enough to pass no comment, as I sat calmly smoking my pipe, trying to exude composure and confidence in our lot. They even begged me to allow them to erect my tent ... I was delighted to conceal my ignorance behind their enthusiasm.

The spuds were peeled and the billies were boiling. To prove that they were boiling, each lad placed a piece of wood against the outside edge of the pot to feel the vibrations. This was classical Scouting lore. That Baden-Powell Manual was truly remarkable, but was not to be good enough for the Tremorfa lads, who had emerged from moulds of doubtful origin, not prepared to accept face value statements. A good example was the stupid paragraph in the Manual which suggested that a good night's sleep was possible on the hard ground, as long as a hole was made to receive your hip bone. That was ridiculous. Personally, with skill, I fashioned a suitable hollow, but my hip was never to hole-out, not even once!

It had taken us a good four hours to assemble the tents and produce the first meal. Actually time was irrelevant. The main objective on my part was to occupy the little angels for every moment of the day in order to reduce them to a state of utter and blissful exhaustion. My real problem was that we had eaten about two days food allocation in one sitting. Each lad was almost capable of eating one loaf per meal! D'rene and I had sadly miscalculated the effect of fresh air on hollow legs and empty stomachs.

The other troops on site had long settled by the time that we came up for intelligent interest and they had, in the meantime, lit a grand central bonfire. We elbowed our way into the group and I was well pleased with the raucous singing of our lot, but took no responsibility for the Tremorfa verbal amendments to B.P.'s suggested renderings. After all, no-one at that stage knew that I was a parson and that we were a Church troop.

We were all tired and needed no urging to hit the blanket. D'rene with diligence and hard-earned skills of putting napkins on the children had taught us how to handle blanket pins. I gladly abandoned the troop to their three tents and left them to find sleep in their own time. They had all night to sort themselves into oblivion.

My tent was precisely three feet and six inches high. I was bigger. Undressing became exhausting. At last, I fell into my blanket and prepared for sleep. I had finished with scouting for the day.

The night was shattered by a noise like thunder. The earth literally quaked beneath my aching bones. I leapt as upright as possible, to an angle of seventy-five degrees as my puny tent wrapped itself about my head. Then my brain got into gear and I understood. The camp site was adjacent to the main line between London and Fishguard and I reckoned that the non-stop, midnight mail train had just missed me by a foot or two. We had barely noticed the noise when we were on our feet. That first night was not good. It was also very cold. I was not a very happy Group Scout Master.

With a sigh, I crawled out into the world at six thirty to thank God for the morning and the lack of rain. That was the only blessing in sight, as our dawn cracked. I had issued instructions that no shoes or stockings were to be worn until after breakfast and the morning dew had gone. Washing was going to be no problem for the Tremorfa lads. Parents make much about soap, drying properly and warm feet. We knew better.

The camp site was neatly sandwiched between the railway and a river. A large sign said "Bathing Prohibited". It went on to talk about pollution and germs, but to our lot, who had swum off the 'beach' at Tremorfa, the water appeared to be crystal clear. No time was wasted with reading. Trunks on, we fell into the freezing water. There was no need for advice from me to wash behind all protuberances. Then we ran around the site, trampling over guy ropes, dripping water, and making sure that no-one overslept. We were remarkably popular!

The fire was still kindled. They were starving again. Water boiled. Cornflakes, bread and marg and quantities of jam were devoured. It was Sunday. We washed up and tidied our area and then I inspected each victim for signs of life. No-one had died during the night. All was well.

There was no way in which I would inflict our bunch on the local Church, so we sat in a circle and said our prayers and sang a hymn with a great sense of freedom. This actually surprised the other troops!

One patrol was left the task of preparing the main meal for the late afternoon, whilst the other two packed sandwiches before I led them off into the country for a six hour hike. This was to be the pattern each day.

For me it was survival, as I drew on my knowledge of the very terrain where I had roamed as a boy. There were small rock faces to climb, streams to dam and paddle in, trees to ascend and acres of ferns for hide and seek. For town lads, it was magic. I was happy, too!

Wednesday was to be the great day. We were all scrubbed and polished. Even the grass was dusted. The billies were boiling for the great arrival. The parents were coming by bus that afternoon for the only visit allowed all week. I was praying for continued sunshine and food parcels.

God bless all mothers! They matched the Berlin airlift. Like panniered donkeys, they brought in supplies for their little darlings. It was the answer to prayer, a modern miracle of the loaves and the fishes. Promptly all fodder was impounded. The rest of the week was bountiful, even though we were to live mainly on cake. Never since have I eaten apple tart for breakfast!

To our utter amazement, we all slept after the first night and there were no complaints. Not a drop of blood was shed. The visit of the parents produced nothing but praise. Mothers pronounced their offspring to be clean, ruddy cheeked and healthy. They sounded surprised. Not one asked to go home. Maybe the thought of eating cake for three days was bribe enough. I believed that we had all grown in stature.

During my years in Tremorfa, there was only to be one more camp, as my time ran out. That second camp was horrendous; it actually poured with rain every day and was not warm enough to dry our clothes. One lad had not been well before we set out for that week, but he insisted that he would cope. He spent most of the week in his blanket on the ground. When his mother came on the Wednesday, she obviously wanted him home, but again he refused and saw the week through. This impressed me, as I knew that he was completely spoiled at home. This was solidarity.

Sadly, when I left Tremorfa, the Scout Group collapsed as my successor showed no interest. In the areas where they have all the good things of life, there is always plenty of leadership, but it is almost impossible to entice that catalyst into places like Tremorfa.

Decades later, when I was in Liverpool working amongst seafarers, I met one of the lads who had shared our camping exploits. He was full of praise for what we had achieved. But, I had learned my lesson. Never again would I involve myself with scouts and camping, because I had realised that we had only survived by good luck. Scouting is a task for the well trained and the expert. The risks in caring for the adventurous young are too great. That ended my Scouting life and I was to hang up my woggle for good.

To my surprise, I had become involved with so much activity that I had forgotten about the problem of how to get started in Tremorfa.

# 10.
# SETTLED

One parson's wife recently hit the headlines of the local paper with 'Mothers' Union of No Value'. It was hardly worth a paragraph as an article, but produced furore in her parish. Her husband had just been appointed to the Parish and he was given rather a cool reception by the ladies. Happily, when we arrived in Tremorfa, D'rene was silent, although she had joined the M.U. in Aberdare and regarded it as a 'grandmothers' union'.

My experience of such a formidable organisation was nothing but gratitude for the excellent work as a support team for almost any possible objective. The ladies of Tremorfa were the proverbial pillars. The truth was that I needed all the help available from any source. Many years later I was to face such groups as the Wigan Women's Gas Federation ... and survived! It is wiser to work with, rather than against, the ladies. Man is really not dominant.

The main social high spot for the Church in Tremorfa was the Christmas Fair. Whatever else it achieved, I had to admit that it enabled us to pull together in roughly the same direction for some months. That alone was of value for a community with little incentive.

The unseen backbone of this great event was an organisation with the basic title of 'The Sewing Guild'. It was an assorted bundle of females, endowed with the minimum of talent, much enthusiasm and an immense capacity for imbibing tea. I baby-sat. For D'rene it was her only night out.

Once a week, for almost the whole year, these dozen sewing experts assembled in the Church vestry and did what they could. Some sported table cloths and indulged themselves in embroidering entwines of Michaelmas daises with the occasional leaf. Each cloth took the twelve months to complete and was then sold for a pittance of its real value and with no reference to the blood, sweat and cups of tea involved in its production. D'rene, with tact, moved in on this group. She was at least half the age of most of them, but was made very welcome.

Our dining room table soon disappeared under mounds of material as D'rene drew patterns for animals and dolls. This was a brave new world for the Sewing Guild. The less adventurous manufactured oven cloths and embroidered sets for dressing tables. New designs were drawn on table cloths, serviettes were cut, threads were pulled, sides machined ... the sweat shops of Bangkok would have been proud of us! D'rene never faltered. The group became animated, as my beloved was accepted as the natural leader, a fact which she has ever denied. Yet another group of folk had been won over.

Tins of food, left over from the Harvest Festival, had been stockpiled for the Christmas Fair. A large cardboard box appeared at the back of the Church for the Sunday worshippers to drop off their tins of peas and beans and all the year's unwanted birthday presents. Recycling was our business ... some of those gifts must have been wandering in and out of our Christmas Fairs for years. As the date drew near, the most impassioned part of the Service was my plea for support. It was a cry from the heart and an unspoken 'Roll on the New Year'.

Protocol had to be learned and strictly observed. I was expected to be endowed with supernatural perception. They assumed that I knew the names of those who had ever run each stall. Even though they expected to be in control, they still waited to be asked. I did my groundwork the only possible way. It was easy. D'rene dropped the odd question at the weekly Sewing Guild and the blueprint was mine.

D'rene was the perfect mole and managed to keep me out of trouble. Over the years, we discovered that D'rene was to help in the kitchen at any function, whilst I avoided all the shots on the platform. My briefing was always complete. Of course, I realised that the system also worked in the opposite direction. If the congregation wanted to convey a thought to me, it homed in via the kitchen telegraph. Thus the pain of a head-on confrontation was avoided and tricky situations were handled with everyone's eyes open. It always paid to be a little devious and it was rarely necessary to discuss any uncomfortable truths, which would only produce discord.

The Christmas Fair was a full day's slog, but in the end it helped to edge the accounts into the black as we survived yet another financial year. Nothing was to be easy in Tremorfa. These were the days before the Wells Organisation, which introduced 'planned giving' into parishes with great success. Tremorfa would have kicked such ideas into touch without much thought and for us the word 'covenant' did not exist.

We could not afford to spend any money on printing, so I became quite versatile at drawing posters on the back of wall paper for the notice board, which we had rescued, restored and painted.

Jumble Sales were an essential means of clothing the old and the young and, in the process, producing about twenty pounds in hard cash at each event. Sacks of old jumble cluttered the vestry as the better quality of the unsold clobber was held back for the next time round. Rubbish was sold for pulp at two shillings a sack. Nothing was to be wasted. Fortunately, I had discovered a fool-proof method of finding new jumble. The cubs and scouts were guaranteed fifty per cent of the proceeds, if they coughed up with the goods. That worked beautifully.

The queue for entry into the Hall, at three pence a head, stretched out on to the main road. The doors were always opened on the dot or they would have been reduced to matchsticks.

The ladies gave no mercy, as they rushed the counters, armed with bags and determination, but I was up to the challenge, using an old valley trick. I had been trained well in Cwmdare.

There was to be a new system of payment. The rule was simple. 'Help yourself'. They did. The jumble was pushed into bags with enthusiasm. The other part of the rule was equally simple. 'Pay at the door!' This was not popular. They had been used to paying for one garment, as two others were lifted during the bargaining. We set up a table like a customs shed. It was amazing how many items were put back as deals were struck. Nothing was above six-pence, but many a blind eye was turned.

My biggest surprise, following a Jumble Sale, was a letter with a cheque for twenty-five pounds. The sender had bought a vase for three pence and was honest enough to state in his letter that it proved to be Viennese glass and of value. I was delighted. Actually, I recalled the particular pot and reckoned that it was over priced at three pence. Thank God for the discerning!

Most Jumbles realised the expected twenty pounds, which was a lot of money and enabled us to meet the quarterly bills, but in a round-about way they helped me to meet people. At last I was able to walk the streets receiving the odd nod and greeting.

Evangelism is to do with the spreading of the 'Good News', but much ground work is required before any word is spoken. If the people have no idea as to who you are, communication is a waste of time. The first step is just to establish a natural friendship.

A great friend of ours was John Eastmond, who happened at that time to sell Wrens Boot Polish for a living. His dictum was to the point.

"If the customers don't like you, they won't buy your polish, even if it is the best in the world! And, you've got to believe that it is the best product in the world or you won't sell a thing."

That was sound advice.

Once Easter and Whitsun were over, the Church calendar went into the doldrums for the twenty-five weeks of Trinity Sundays. I knew all about the theological thinking behind this arrangement, but it produced little colour for the congregation. A more positive objective was needed to discover if there was any life in Tremorfa. It felt like a search for life before death, because nothing happened in Tremorfa in the summer to prove that anyone cared about anyone or any thing. My only excuse was that I was young, naive and possibly stupid. A wiser man might have just dug his garden, enjoyed the sunshine and let the world go about its business.

I proposed that we held a Summer Fete. The Church Committee met this with silence, whilst I was dreaming of an outstanding success. In a strange way, that happened.

The rest of the Parish of Roath paid no attention to our efforts in Tremorfa and a proposal that we were about to send a rocket to the moon would have passed unnoticed. Apart from the quarter page that we claimed in the Parish Magazine to publicise our activities, we might just as well have lived in outer space. The advantage was that we could order our own affairs and that was what we did.

My main supporter for the Summer Fete was a young man called Bob Morgan. He was an ordinand, training for the priesthood with the Mirfield Fathers in Leeds. Out of term, he worked on the Cardiff buses, but found time to help me in my hour of need.

Many years later, Bob was not only the Vicar of Ely, not too easy an assignment, but was also the Chairman of the Cardiff City Council. We were not to agree on his mix of religion and active politics when we met thirty years later, although I applauded his endeavours to improve the living standards of his parishioners. However, Bob and I had more important matters to worry about than the future of a City of half a million! The Summer Fete was to be our baby.

Together we built the various stalls and stands. We devised ball games and activities for the youngsters and, above all, a gambling Wheel of Fortune, all guaranteed to do the trick on the great day. There was little support as we strove, but many promised to help on the field on the Saturday. That field was the rough piece of ground alongside the Church. It had been turned into allotments in wartime, remaining derelict ever since, and it was a major task to flatten the mounds and cut the grass. Bob and I developed blisters with blisters on them. No-one seemed interested enough to leap to our aid. We needed publicity. We scattered the railings with exotic wall-paper posters and prayed for sunshine. Parsons are expected to pray.

The sun beamed on the invasion of kids and dogs as the decibel level rose on that fun-packed afternoon. Three-legged scrambles and egg and spoon dashes and thirty yard sack race fiascos were loved by all. Cake stalls and white elephant and jumble competed with hoopla and darts and roll-a-penny. Tea and pop washed down mounds of fairy cakes. Towards the end of the afternoon, the more robust and solid confections were sold to the highest bidder. Most were rescued by those who had made them, lest they appeared to be unsaleable! Very little money was spent and lots of prizes had to be given. All participants had to win something. One passing local rattled the church railings with his walking stick to get my attention. He thrust half-a-crown into my hand. I felt rich.

The total take, at the end, was a massive twenty pounds and we were all delighted. It had been a fantastic afternoon of fun and hard work.

The following year I had left Tremorfa and in my next Parish the fete we organised, with far less effort and ten times the support, produced over a thousand pounds. But that year in the hot summer in Tremorfa, for one day we all had fun.

I know the old saying about the Lord helping those who help themselves, but sometimes the Divine assistance would seem to be somewhat uneven. I did not complain.

*St. Philip's, Tremorfa*

# 11.
# TOGETHERNESS

A little knowledge of drains is essential for the parson, as he works in the vineyard to the glory of God. I proved this over many years of bitter apprenticeship. The grounding was started in Tremorfa.

Our new house appeared to be very large and extremely comfortable after the squeeze of the flat in Partridge Road. As the house dried out, pools of water collected on the Marley tiles in the lounge and trickles of moisture coursed down the bedroom walls. We were assured that all this was normal and would disappear when we put some heat into the house. This was sound advice, although heat required money. Cracks appeared in ceilings, the skirtings moved away from the walls and there were positive gaps under the window sills. We were assured, yet again, that this was normal. We responded with mops and plaster and wallpaper. Then came the smell.

Drains always draw attention to themselves when it is too late. That point was proved as I lifted the manhole cover outside the back door. I could tell an emergency when it hit me on the nose. D'rene posed the question.

"What do you propose to do?"

"Don't know."

Decisiveness is essential in a crisis and most men are awake to the fact that doing nothing is a sort of decision. Men like to plan ahead, to consider and discuss, to perambulate, ponder and peruse ... above all, we need time. I knew nothing about drains.

"Why don't you borrow some rods!"

D'rene knew the man. Women are trained to organise men.

"Don't worry. Leave it to me."

Determination set in, when I realised that it was my problem. Rods were borrowed and I set to work with energy and little knowledge. That is a fatal combination of forces. The rest of the family had withdrawn into the house, as they distanced themselves from my expertise.

Quickly I made a great discovery. It is better to tackle such a problem, not from the offending manhole, but from the one next down from the natural flow. You would think that Thomas Aquinas might have included that information, even as an addendum, in one of his Treatises; after all, he tried to cover every other snag which God had thrown at mankind.

I was not having a happy experience, in spite of my eventual discovery of the half brick, which was the cause of our little dilemma.

"Have a bath!"

This was D'rene's contribution, although she had not quite finished.

"Wash the rods before you take them back."

Drains do not exude happiness.

There was more to come. Word by this time had gone forth that Evans was a crack hand with the rods, like a twentieth century Moses. I must have been stupid enough to refer to my exploits when making a glib parsonical point during a sermon. Such knowledge is noted by the faithful, although they are endowed with the ability to ignore all theological shafts of wisdom.

The Church Hall drains had reached a perilous condition. Even the local canines were avoiding us. Rods were again produced and a small posse of parishioners stood by to offer advice. They all awaited my response and I knew that I was at the sharp end!

My eventual discovery was that a block of margarine had mysteriously caused a major thrombosis. The posse became engaged in a discussion about the likely source of the trouble. Half bricks were easier to remove. I received no thanks and concluded that drains and loving your neighbour are not compatible.

So I had learned a little about drains, though decades were to pass before I had completed my training. The final lesson was a long time coming and should have been obvious from the start. It was simple. "Get some other sucker to do it!".

Meanwhile in Tremorfa, I was still serving my apprenticeship.

The house stood on a large plot of land best described as a jungle. The contractor had removed the obvious rubble and promptly departed. There had been no provision for landscaping or even basic levelling of the mountainous sods. That was left to me. The coal house ... such fuel was the only source of heat at that time ... was large enough for ten hundred weight and a shovel. The result was that my bike stood naked against the back wall, surrounded by bramble bushes and mud. My brain told me that I was in need of a garden shed.

Happily I chanced upon a neighbour in the act of demolishing a decrepit looking bundle of firewood, which could be recognised, with the eye of despair, as a garden shed. He was about to burn it and erect a new one. The wreck was mine.

"Are you sure you want it?"

In fairness to him, I did hesitate for a moment

"Just what I was looking for."

His look said it all.

"Take this tin of old nails!"

"There's a lot of them."

"You'll need them!"

The 'shed' was easy to move as it fell apart, at a touch, into handy, take-away timber sizes.

No-one could have guessed that the wood I casually carried through the street was actually anything in particular. With great skill and that abundance of rusty nails, I fabricated a shed. It must have been a job well done because it retained the outline of a shed for five years, bending before each westerly gust with dignity. The next task was to be the garden.

One afternoon, I returned from a session of house visiting to find D'rene, blackened, shattered and in need of comfort. These were pre-valium days and no-one had heard of 'counselling'. The basic approach to bombing, house destruction and the odd mental crack-up was the phrase, 'Get on with it!' D'rene needed help.

That lunchtime, one side of the garden had been entirely covered by six foot high brambles. They must have been a tremendous sight as they disappeared. Stephen was at the staggering stage and hard to pin into a pram. Apparently he squealed with delight, when his mother put a match to the brambles. She had not realised that, whilst the outside of the bushes was green, the inside comprised decades of dry tinder.

The blaze had, apparently, been beautiful with flames house-high, shooting flying, burning ash heavenwards. It had been completely out of control and had threatened to set Tremorfa ablaze. I arrived home, just as she was beating at the dying embers and emerging from a slight attack of hysteria. Words failed me, but she had saved me hours of toil. All that was left was to dig for victory.

The plan was to put as much as possible to grass, so I approached the Vicar for the cost of the seed. Tremorfa had no means or history of meeting any expenses incurred by the clergy. We provided our own stamps and stationery and any other office equipment. My request for seed caused alarm as it fell upon stony ground. The matter had to be discussed and then I was asked to put the request in writing. I was proud of my postscript, which noted that the Vicarage garden had been professionally landscaped the previous year. I got my seed.

I swung my pick and beavered away happily, levelling the virgin land, but all was not well. The more I used the rake and manoeuvred the soil, the higher a large lump of concrete emerged. I dug down and around and failed to shift it. For weeks I had laboured and buried stones. This monster was the last straw. It was obviously the responsibility of the contractor. I put my request politely.

To my consternation, a man who must have been knocking eighty arrived, armed with a spade, which looked too heavy for him. His solution was simple. He dug a very large hole alongside the monster and with ease tumbled it in. This is how we lesser mortals learn.

My vegetable plot was my pride and joy. Each section was bounded by a strip of lawn and could be worked without standing on the soil. Everything grew and we enjoyed our greens. They were also enjoyed by Stephen's tortoise, as it set about devouring my seed bed. One night that animal, in spite of a yellow star painted on its shell, disappeared into the long grass around the church. I did not search with diligence.

One small triangle remained untouched, surrounded by a concrete path, near the front door. It was the size of a dining table, but full of stone and builder's rubbish. This was my last task in the garden. As I dug and cleaned, I listened to the radio as Blackpool in extra time won the F.A. Cup and, at last, Stanley Matthews received a medal. Mother-in-law arrived with dahlias and the garden was complete.

Gardeners in Tremorfa had been observing all my efforts and yet another bond of friendship had been forged. On house visits, the men now asked me to come and look at their back gardens. Advice was freely given and cuttings handed over with pride. At last I was allowed to chat to the male population, but only those with green fingers.

Two conifers graced either side of the front door, but just before one Christmas one of them went walk-about and presumably became a Yuletide tree.

The word 'ecumenism' had just been coined and was only appearing in discussions when we all wished to impress each other. Brave things were said about visions of the future and dreams of the togetherness of all the Churches. At the time it all seemed a little irrelevant.

Each denomination had set up its stall, knew what it had to sell and needed no advice from outsiders. Ecumenism was a threat. Discussion was only an excuse to display our own authority and reveal in the process the shortcomings of all the other Churches. We thought that we possessed the true faith and were willing to welcome all the others to join us ... on our terms!

Bishop William Temple had disturbed us by his statement that, if you really believe in ecumenism, then you must be prepared to accept the death of your own church as you know it. He was asking too much.

We could look no further than being happy for any group to come alongside us on our terms. This was not as depressing as at first might appear, because we were all starting at the right place by looking at ourselves in terms of others. There is no other place to start.

The cynics amongst us saw the battle for survival of just ourselves. Certainly that was my position. There was no way in Tremorfa in which I could make contact with any other denomination. I was on my own.

One small attempt to tell folk that we existed produced a startling reaction, and it placed our thoughts on ecumenism into perspective. I had printed a leaflet with the times of our Services, a word of welcome and an invitation for the youngsters to join our youth activities. A select band of workers scattered them to every house on the estate. It was an error of judgement.

The very next day after the delivery of my pamphlets, I was summoned to the Vicarage. I had committed the ultimate ecclesiastical crime! I had trespassed over the boundary of a neighbouring Anglican Parish.

I failed to see the enormity of my actions. Apparently a mythical boundary line had been drawn over the marsh land, which had become Tremorfa. This line had been created in the last century and remained legally correct. Then a railway line had chopped off a triangular corner. That triangle was not in my patch! It belonged to the Parish of St. Saviour in Splott. Incidentally, the only school serving the children in my area was also in that triangle. The fact that the clergy of St. Saviour's were not involved in that school made no difference to the principle that I had no right to visit or make any contact.

So I was officially ticked off, even though Gwynno smiled and agreed that it was all a nonsense ... including the fact that the clergy of St. Saviour's would have had to walk through my area in order to reach their golden triangle! No wonder the problems of ecumenism were not top of our worry list! I wrote my apology, as directed, to the offended Vicar and continued on my merry way.

Many of the faithful walked from Tremorfa to worship in that other Parish and that was their privilege. I assumed that the Vicar of St. Saviour's also visited them. At the time, all this trivia seemed to be very important.

The value of my Tremorfa experience was proved twenty years later. When I arrived in the Parish of Rainhill, on Merseyside, I met the neighbouring Vicar of Prescot, John Mills, and we readily agreed that we would ignore boundaries, apart from any legal requirement where marriages were concerned. We had no problems over that arrangement. The real lesson was that, if we cannot work together in our own Church, there is little hope of working with the other Churches.

# 12.
# PER ARDUA

The old Cardiff airport was certainly within my patch, even though there were no longer any aircraft and little signs of any former glory. All that remained was a collection of wartime Nissen huts and an aura of decay and neglect. Nothing seemed to be happening there. I felt sad that no longer was the sound of Merlins to be heard, as the Spitfires came into land.

My memories took me back to clay pigeon shooting on the range, when the airfield was in use by the R.A.F. during the war. That range had been set on the edge of the River Rumney at the far end of the runway. It was there that I had my first flight in a Domine Rapide, when I was a member of the University Air Squadron. I still recall flying past Nash Point, St. Donat's Castle and my beloved Southerndown with its exciting cliffs. Perhaps, that was why I had wandered into the airfield a decade later with my dog collar, although it was part of my area of responsibility and I was inquisitive.

All activity on the airfield was being phased out and no-one foresaw a future for the site. Eventually, some years on, a Rover Car Factory was built, but even that was short lived. Now, forty years later, there is an official 'gypsy site' on the spot where I used to take the scouts to light their camp fires and dream dreams. That site is full of cars and caravans and is as mucky as ever, except on the day that Princess Anne paid a formal visit and the local council workers moved in to clear the debris. Back in the early fifties, the airfield was all doom and gloom and yet it was the very place where I was to find a way forward in personal survival in Tremorfa.

Amongst the Nissen huts I came across the premises of an Air Training Squadron. One evening I dropped in to see what they were doing. I was turning the clock back because, when the A.T.C. was formed in the early days of the war, I had joined the Squadron in Bridgend County Grammar School, then graduated to the University Air Squadron before eventually entering the Royal Air Force for training as a pilot. Naturally I was somewhat excited at what I had found on my own door-step.

The welcome was tremendous. The Commanding Officer was a gentle character called Clifford Turner, whose daily work was heading a building company famous in South Wales, particularly for building the Brangwyn Hall in Swansea. Both Clifford and his delightful wife, Cora, were to become close friends until their deaths forty years later. There was another amiable character, Alun Emlyn Jones. Alun, like me, was ex-aircrew and was involved in the world of shipping. I was to take my driving test in his Vauxhall Cresta and from him purchase our very first car, a 1932 Austin Seven. The third officer was John Bonas, who was in the insurance world of General Accident. This remarkable trio made it quite clear that I was needed and that there could be no refusal. If they felt that they needed me, there was no question but that I needed them. This was the group which kept my soul alive in my five years in Tremorfa.

Almost on the spot I became the Squadron Chaplain, which involved me with about fifty young men, aged between twelve and eighteen. I also was asked to give lectures on the Theory of Flight and Meteorology. I wondered what the youngsters made of a parson indulging himself in such heavenly matters! Naturally, we held Padre's Sessions and a series of Any Questions with the lads themselves forming a panel ... it was lively and popular. They opened my eyes to their thoughts and needs, their doubts and questions. This was pure gold. I was well used by the Squadron.

It was suggested that I might be a more versatile member of the Unit if I were commissioned. The Examining Board met at the Royal Auxiliary Air Force Station at Ely in Cardiff. That Station, in common with all the other Auxiliary Units, which had formed the backbone of the defence of the country at the beginning of the war, was shortly to be wound up and I still recall the party when we used up the Mess Funds in the customary manner. The Board was happy about my background, so yet again I was able to wear my uniform. The expected remarks were made during the interview about a Padre with pilot's wings and I was inevitably dubbed 'the sky pilot'.

My Vicar understood what it was all about and gave me every encouragement. Apart from the normal weekly drills, I was expected to spend seven days with the Squadron each year at a Summer Camp. I was relieved that D'rene thoroughly approved of my activities.

All of this was really the beginning of a form of ministry, which continued alongside my normal dog collar business until I was fifty-five and over the age for a Service Chaplain.

Thanks to my work with the Air Training Corps. and then some years later in Liverpool with the Royal Naval Reserve, I was able to meet men and women from all walks of life and from every level of education, as we were joined together in a common bond of interest. Doors opened wherever I went.

Most of my fellow clergy never seemed to understand the value of this form of ministry. Maybe they only saw the uniform and therefore missed the whole point of the exercise. Being a Padre is not the easiest of tasks. It may open doors, but you still have to win your way into the lives of your companions.

As the Padre, I was able to meet people who generally had little, if any, church contacts and in some cases had no time for a clergyman. In a strange way, the Padre is not seen as a parson because he does not conform with the stereotyped image of 'a man of the cloth'. He is part of the team. I saw that my task was to become a friend and confidant. This took time. Above all I learned the art of knowing when to speak and when to be silent and when to depart. These were vital lessons for a Padre to take on board. Friendships were made to last a lifetime and, as the years went by, I became the personal chaplain to many families. Perhaps that was what it was all about. It was a ministry to the individual and not to a worshipping body. When eventually I moved to Merseyside, I easily transferred from the Royal Air Force to become a Royal Naval Reserve Chaplain and, in that role, continued for some twenty years.

Whilst attached to the A.T.C. in Tremorfa, we set out with the cadets to stay at many R.A.F. Stations. This was work which involved much thought and time, and inevitably widened my horizons and broadened my humour.

On one such R.A.F. Station, I was appointed the Officer of the Day, which involved much walking about looking as fierce as possible, inspecting quarters and checking the quality of the food. Some wag in the Administration Office allocated a Warrant Officer Priest to accompany me and we received appropriate comments, as we perambulated our 'parish'.

*"Why should England tremble!"*

There was one moment when we might have met our Maker. Our C.O., Clifford Turner, with all his devoted staff aboard, turned the wrong way and, to our consternation, we proceeded in his car up the main runway of that Coastal Command Station in Cornwall. There followed a fine display of flashing lights and fireworks, as we hastened on our way. We were met at the far end by a gentleman with a very fine turn of phrase!

On another occasion, for some strange reason I spent the day in charge of the Station Assault Course. I was really enjoying the sunshine, whilst the professionals about me put the victims through their agony. I was rudely awakened, when one young airman missed a rope, took off into the air and landed head first into a ditch, which sadly chanced to be full of oil. We all moved quickly to extract him; it was not the time for delegation. That evening the Group Captain cornered me, retold the story to his admirers and suggested that I stuck to water for Baptisms.

The Suez affair raised many an eyebrow in the Parish. The week that we invaded the Canal Zone chanced to coincide with my disappearance in uniform for a week's camp with the A.T.C. Some folk in Tremorfa thought that I had been called up for the defence of the Realm, although I am not sure what my contribution might have been.

Whilst away I naturally telephoned D'rene each night to make sure that all was well with the family ... Jane had arrived by this time and was making herself useful! My roars of laughter were not too well received by D'rene, as she described how Jane had placed a plant pot into the fish bowl. The result had been a large puddle of mud in which the two fish were doing the back stroke on the white Indian carpet. I dared not tell her of my brave endeavours to protect the Queen and the Country.

Because of my contacts with the A.T.C., I was invited to join a group called the Arkaves. All this arose from my friendship with Alun Emlyn Jones and was a fascinating episode in my life.

After the war, Alun along with other friends was looking for ways of augmenting his income and he hit on a novel idea. It was all to do with School Canteens and ready-cleaned spuds and carrots. Alun and his mates, all ex-aircrew, set up an organisation to clean the vegetables, put them into churns and deliver them daily to the canteens. This business took off to such an extent that the group had to call upon their wives to help with the chores. Eventually, the sheer boredom of the mundane activity got to them all. Apart from the evening's spud-bashing, they had their daily work to keep them occupied. It was all too much; so the business was sold as a 'going concern'.

That was when the partners made the discovery that they actually missed the fun and challenge of their evening work with the potatoes. Something had to be done to keep the companionship alive. From the 'ready-cleaned vegetables' title they took the first three letters, 'r.c.v.', turned them into 'R.K.V.' and produced the name Arkaves.

The Arkaves became a small group of like-minded men, all of whom had been flying during the war. I was invited to join. The numbers were limited to fifteen. We all met once a month in a pub, which each member in turn nominated. The fare was sandwiches and ale or whatever. The objective, initially, had been just to enjoy each other's company. It was not enough. New thoughts evolved.

During the summer months, we adopted an Old People's Home and, once a week, we took 'inmates' for an evening run into the country with a stop at a favourite watering hole. My venue was always the Three Cups at Moulton with its minstrel's gallery and chicken in the basket, which was all the vogue at that time. We never failed to please, although my ancient Austin Seven was not called upon to provide any transport.

In the winter, each member organised a fund raising event in his own area and by this means we were able to provide a number of television sets in some of the Homes. This was a long way from peeling potatoes, but kept the spirit of co-operation with each other fully alive and hopefully did a little good.

When eventually I was to leave South Wales for the delights of Merseyside, my name was deleted from the membership of the Arkaves and, as a departing 'vegetable' and because of my accent, I was then described as a 'leek'. It had all been great fun.

# 13.
# ITCHY FEET

The production of Snow White and the Seven Dwarfs in Cwmdare had left scars, but as time passed the memories of the fun had erased the pain. In Tremorfa, I discovered that I was still more than interested in amateur dramatics, which really ought not to be surprising as any act of worship involves movement, sound, colour, lighting, all the ingredients of the theatre.

Even our tin-sheeted church could produce an atmosphere, sufficient to work on the sensibilities of the congregation. Our candles flickered in the down draughts, as I followed the robed choir up the aisle at the start of Evensong. I was dressed in a splendidly coloured cope with its gold lining, whilst two freshly scrubbed, robed, acolytes, carrying candles, flanked me on either side. We sang lustily with more decibels than finesse. Our organist was good enough to tease first class sounds out of our tired organ. We could boast that our choir members with their strange assortment of ill-fitting robes did their best with what God had given them. The congregation kept pace as well as they could with far greater numbers in attendance than most churches can muster today. Everyone was dressed in Sunday best and we all did what we could. However, there was just one little problem which would not go away.

My patience had been trained to be long suffering, fully corked and muted, but in the end even the milk of human kindness can turn sour. I was at the utmost of my cool. All was not well. My problem was one gentleman in the congregation with an exceptionally large voice, which even endangered the roof. Sadly, I became aware that he was in a battle to the death with the organist, who had eased him out of the choir prior to my arrival. The contest was to do with the speed of our singing. He sat on the back row of the nave and bellowed at treble forte at least half a beat ahead of the organ and the congregation. My subtle hints and pointed suggestions were not working. One evening, along with the congregation, I had had enough.

I stopped the farce in the middle of a hymn. The congregation was asked to sit. I marched down the length of the nave.

"Charlie, we've had enough of this nonsense. We cannot go on as we are."

"What's the problem?"

"Please stop singing!"

He did. Then, to my complete surprise, he continued to attend the Services. I congratulated him on his understanding. With persuasion, he became an altar server and, in two ticks, he was the Master of Ceremonies. No longer was there time for him to sing, and peace descended upon us. My respect for Charlie had truly grown.

There is no way in which you can relax in the face of any such difficulty; you can guarantee that in the midst of a struggle for a solution, another person has been waiting in the wings to deputise for the miscreant. Salvage one sinner at your peril, because the next problem is around the corner. Chatting over the silencing of the over-zealous singer, I discovered that he had been 'removed' from a number of churches and that my predecessor had also tried, but failed, to boot him out! Being a Christian has its problems.

Actually, Charlie had not been entirely wrong, as I thought that many a hymn, which should have bounced along, had been reduced to a dirge. He had really been fighting my battle. On reflection, my actions deserved no accolade and I had won nothing. All that I had achieved was to place him in a position to issue directions to the young servers. His stage whispers were piercing. What should have been a time of complete silence was just what Charlie waited for.

"Shift the altar missal!"

This would prompt a server to struggle to his feet with all the eyes of the congregation upon him. Charlie was in charge.

"Not you! Kneel down!"

We all waited for the next instruction for the other server.

"Psst! Shift yourself!"

Then I would turn to face the congregation and utter these words with a bit of a smile.

"The peace of the Lord be always with you"

Charlie always responded treble-forte.

"And with you!"

Some things in life you just have to accept as normal.

Theatrical asides may have been part of the Service, but I felt the need to introduce drama, as a means of communication. The obvious actors were the Sunday School scholars. This would also ensure a good following in the pews and was a fair ploy, as Christian teaching must find its way into the homes and, for the most of the children, their parents had no contact with the church since their marriages. My scheme was a way for them to return without being embarrassed. I got to work.

The Sunday School teachers were happy to co-operate. It had to be simple. There are no better stories than those in the Bible and all that was required was to put them into dialogue form and then relate the theme to everyday life in Tremorfa. The Gospel parables and miracles are already in story form. They all have good 'punch' lines and needed little adaptation.

There had to be a good narrator and two or three other voices. Men volunteered to handle the lighting and they erected a platform, which was the stage. The readers huddled together on the pulpit steps, out of sight of the congregation, and also handled the record player for the background music.

My aim was to use as many teen-agers as possible. Boy always wants to meet girl! The actors were asked to mime everything on the stage. Each production ended with a verse of a hymn, which was then taken up by the congregation. Nothing was to last more than fifteen minutes. The first rehearsal for the evening's performance was held after the morning communion. The dress rehearsal was during Sunday School. Costumes were a happy mixture of curtains, sheets and scarves. It became natural to produce plays for Christmas, Easter and for the Sundays in Lent. There was no lack of volunteers, and the congregation was delighted to be spared a sermon. The Gospel message was, of course, being conveyed without pain to anyone, except that D'rene had to keep an eye on the sheets, curtains and scarves.

I found that sermons were difficult to collate and, all too often, I resorted to the books on my shelves. There was advice in abundance, which often resulted in a long suffering congregation enduring tedious theological discourses with no real beginning, an unintelligent middle and a long-searched-for end. I was lucky that I was not competing with television. No-one openly objected to either content or length. Many must have enjoyed the peace of not listening. This worked, as long as my final burst was loud, clear and obvious. This gave the organist enough time to collect himself and switch on the blower, at which the sleepers would open an eye to see what the disturbance was. The last hymn and collection released the victims for the chat show. Many sat for half an hour with their friends. There was no hurry to go home and it was important that there was a chance to talk.

Years were to pass before I felt that I was able to 'stand up, speak up and shut up' with any real confidence. The greatest test lay well ahead, when I learned that a two minute talk during Divisions in the Royal Naval Reserve would concentrate the mind and I discovered how to make a point with a smile and then ram it home with effect.

"Thank you for a lovely sermon."

I realised that remark meant little as it probably resulted from the hearer selecting what she wanted to hear.

"What a load of rubbish!"

That was never mouthed, but might have been more helpful. The one vital factor that came home to me was that, if I could not hold in my head the thought I was trying to untangle, it would not reach any other head.

The real sadness about Tremorfa was that, whilst I was becoming well known in the area, D'rene and I were not to make many lasting personal friends. D'rene was busy with Stephen and, when Jane arrived one Saturday afternoon by courtesy of the Queen Alexandra's nurses, life went up a tempo. She was born at home. Father-in-law, young Stephen and I sat at the bottom of the stairs as Jane was making herself known to the world ... we prayed for D'rene's mother to cut her shopping short and come to our rescue. Men are not much good in that kind of emergency!

About three years on, Martin was to arrive and then we felt that we were living in one of Dr. Barnado's Homes. D'rene still reckons that she washed nappies for seven years! The washing line was always at full blow, flying at least a dozen surrender signals each day.

Money was desperately short. D'rene's parents never failed to support, knitting and sewing and bringing along some home cooking most Saturdays. Like many folk at that time, we passed clothes on and down the line.

Once I summoned up the courage and put our difficulties to the Vicar. He admitted that he was ashamed of the paucity of the monthly stipend, but the levels were set by the Diocesan authority and, if he were to increase our salaries, the Parish would lose the grants which were received for the payment of curates. Catch 22 had not been written, but we were in it. Decades later my main memories of Tremorfa concern the struggle to survive.

Across the road lived two friendly ladies, Nellie Sullivan and her companion. They seemed pleased to talk to D'rene and gave presents to the children. They both chanced to be Roman Catholics, which probably helped to create a warmth, as we shared the feeling of isolation in our community. R.C.s were comparatively thin on the ground in Wales. They had adopted us. Nellie was a chiropodist, took one look at D'rene's feet and acquired a patient for the rest of her life.

David Thomas, a fellow curate, with his wife Marian, looked after the neighbouring area of St. Agnes and we became great friends. David was to become the Vicar of St. Saviour's, Splott, years ahead, and sadly died a few weeks after Marian was given replacement hips by the famous Doctor Charnley in Wrightington. Maybe our friendship started in Tremorfa, when they came for afternoon tea and departed after lunch on the following day ... we must have believed in the joy of conversation!

Peter and Phyllis Davies could only be friends. Peter was the local policeman. Like us, they both felt out on a limb in Tremorfa. Our children also helped to cement our contact. After a few years, they departed to live in a new estate at Rumney. We helped to dig their garden, which was akin to quarrying. The first Christmas Eve, after their move, I popped in to wish them well and exchange presents and was offered a plate of chitterlings. I did not like their appearance.

"Do you actually eat these?"

"They're lovely. Try a piece"
"What are they?"
"The inside of a pig!"
"How fascinating."

I never did try them and never will. Every Christmas Eve, we now telephone each other and chitterlings always come into the conversation.

Today, when I wallow in nostalgia, I find it hard to fathom the perplexity of Tremorfa. Occasionally in recent years we have driven through the estate and there time seems to have stood still. The streets about the church look the same with no new houses. Our old home appears to be no different, apart from the conifer by the front door, which is now as high as the house, but had been bought as a miniature plant. The only real alteration is the new church, replacing my tin tabernacle. Perhaps, one day, I will stop and have the courage to peep inside to glimpse the ghosts of the past and stick a pin into the bubble of my nostalgia.

I could not pretend that we were to stay over-long in Tremorfa. Gwynno had been right to suggest that five years would be a long sentence, even though naturally at first it was a sort of Shangri-la. Gwynno left the Parish to become the Archdeacon of Llandaff and was replaced by Eric Roberts. Eric in time was to become the Bishop of St. David's. Once again, there was no difficulty in working together, as the new Vicar showed little desire to venture into my part of his vineyard. In fairness, the Parish of Roath was so vast that no new Vicar could possibly avoid delegation. However, all the curates realised that every new incumbent needs to build up his own support team and that the time had come to consider a move.

One avenue of escape was, obviously, to go back into the Royal Air Force as a Chaplain. I applied for an interview. This meant that all cards had to be disclosed, so I informed my Vicar and also Bishop Glyn Simon. At that time, it was regarded as an act of disloyalty to leave the Church in Wales for pastures new, but I was prepared to do just that and commit the ultimate crime.

At last, I was summoned to the R.A.F. Moral Leadership Centre at Dowsdale Court to spend a few days and be assessed as a potential Chaplain. My spirits were high, as I was well received and met a number of R.A.F. Chaplains with whom I chatted about the future. Life had changed dramatically from the Royal Air Force of my memories, which really ought not to have been such a surprise. When I thought about my life in Tremorfa, 'service life' seemed to be cocooned into an artificial world with little purpose and too set a structure. Not entirely convinced, I returned to down-town Cardiff to await the verdict.

Weeks were to pass before I was informed that, whilst I was acceptable, there were to be large cuts in the manning levels of all the armed forces, which would result in a 'cut back' in the Chaplaincy Branch. Oddly we were not disappointed, but pleased that we were to avoid the implications of the move. A letter arrived from Gwynno, the Archdeacon of Llandaff, suggesting that God might even work through the Chaplain in Chief of the Royal Air Force and that I should persevere where I was for a while longer. I could not argue with those sentiments.

We can all remember trivial events which surround a traumatic happening. I was up to my elbows in the sink cleaning myriads of shallots, which had been drying off in the garden in preparation for pickling. The jars were lined up, the vinegar and spices all set to go, my eyes were weeping, when the Vicar arrived. My father had died. Apparently, he had called at the surgery to receive his Autumn flu jab and had died of a heart attack in the waiting room. No words can describe the loss of a father.

It is no surprise that, whilst as a parson, I had learned to cope with the sadness of bereavement in a sympathetic and necessarily detached way, when the pain is personal, all professionalism disappears. I cannot forget the time when I visited my mother in Bridgend Hospital, where she was obviously recovering from a hernia operation and, as I approached the bed, I burst into tears. The death of a father removes an important person out of your life and, even though I had been standing on my own two feet for many years, for the first time I realised that I had come of age.

Almost immediately after the R.A.F episode, D'rene and I visited Stoke-on-Trent to see if our future lay there. D'rene later confessed that she was convinced that it would not have been the right move even when we were on the train heading for the place! The reception was kind and after a meal at the Vicarage, we met the two church wardens. Their opening remarks seemed a bit unnecessary.

"We're blunt folk around here and call a spade a spade."

I was not sure what they were trying to say to me or what image they had of themselves, because the pair of them were the most gentle of characters. They offered me a job on the spot.

I slept badly that night in Stoke and awoke in the morning, soaked with perspiration. My head throbbed. I was not well. On the way home, by train, we both felt that there was little to discuss as we knew that the Parish and all those smoking chimneys were not for us. It was an easy decision. I just went to bed with influenza and forgot about it.

By this time, I felt that I had learned my trade as a parson, although the moment you think that, life springs another surprise to cut you down to size. I carried on visiting.

In one home, there was a daughter aged seven. She suffered encephalitis and lay on the living room floor with her enlarged head resting on a cushion. After a number of calls at the house, I had been accepted by her parents as a friend. The conversation was invariably about Daphne. It was not an easy situation, fearing the inevitable question, "Why us?". I was unsure what my reply might have been. On one visit, as I walked through the kitchen to the back door with Daphne's father alongside me, I expressed my sense of pity.

"You are all very brave."

He turned sharply on me and put me firmly in my place.

"You've missed the point. We regard it as a privilege to care for Daphne and we'll do it to the end."

It was stern lesson in the understanding of the word 'love'.

In another home, I was a regular visitor, taking communion for a young man of eighteen, who was dying of T.B. It was too late for him. The wonder drugs were almost with us, but all that I could do was to hold his hand and convey what strength I could.

"I'm not afraid to die!"

There was no way to avoid a discussion. Perhaps, I was the only person with whom he could be totally honest. He had to help me!

"I've no idea what lays ahead of me ... if it's nothing, it's better than this."

"Why don't we leave it in God's hands?"

This was my typical, rather pathetic, parsonical remark.

"I've done that a long time ago!"

Again, I had been cut down to size and should have listened to him, as he handled his problem in his way. Later I realised, as new drugs came on the market, that another year might have saved his life. I was to continue learning for the rest of my ministry.

Almost next door to us was a thirty-year old man, an ex-soldier, whose days were numbered. He never talked about his experiences and it took that remarkable film, 'The Bridge over the River Kwai', before we in this country began to understand the implications of the Japanese conquest, which led to the building of the Burma Railway. It was said that every sleeper on the railway cost the life of a prisoner of war. I sat alongside this man, who was taking ten years to die. He never complained. When I found him, he was almost too weak to talk. I was beginning to understand that words from me were not necessary and would have been of little value. However, he did ask one question of me.

"Are you a friend of God?"

I gave what I thought was an honest answer.

"Yes."

He just nodded and put his hand into mine. That was all that he seemed to want of me, as his days faded. I trust that it was enough

On the infallible, ecclesiastical grape-vine, I had gleaned that Edwin Davies, who was the Curate at Llandaff Cathedral, had been appointed to be Vicar of Llantrisant. When I had gone up to Cardiff University, Edwin had been in his last year at College, before going on to read Theology at St. Michael's at Llandaff. I knew him well. He had been Curate at the Cathedral for almost nine years and was part of the fabric. D'rene urged me to make contact with the Dean and to put my name into the arena. We discussed this long and hard, as I felt that it was 'bad form' to push yourself forward. D'rene was right.

My telephone call to the Deanery told me that the Dean was not available and I left my name. Arriving home for lunch after my morning calls, D'rene said that the Dean had asked that I call him. To my surprise, he seemed pleased that I had made the first move and we arranged to meet the next day.

Llandaff was the other side of the city from Tremorfa, in every sense. We gave our Austin Seven an extra polish, as we set out that next day.

That car had been the proud possession of Alun Emlyn Jones and he had sold it to us for forty pounds. Driving it was an experience. Alun had helped me pass the Driving Test in his posh Vauxhall Cresta, but actually I had been driving at the age of fifteen. No-one seemed to care at that time, as I used to drive from Llanharan to Bridgend each morning, me on the way to Grammar School and Dad on the way to the County Court.

No car has ever matched that Austin Seven. Above all it was the first car and it was ours! D'rene was pregnant for the third time and, with impossible contortions, had cleverly fitted an old army blanket on the underside of the roof. It was amazing what could be done with an army blanket ... D'rene had made a dressing gown out of two of them for our large policeman friend, Peter Davies. I had polished every bit of the car for the journey to Llandaff. We aimed to arrive in style.

David Thomas had expertly fixed two rear indicating lights, some months before, as the Law had just decreed that the old, pop-out, orange trafficators were illegal and obsolete, even though for that age of car they were rather a novelty.

At five miles an hour, the front wheels wobbled dramatically, but I had learned to drive through the judder as though through the sound barrier. A friendly mechanic had given me sound advice.

"Don't grease the king pins."

"No problem!"

That advice was followed, as I had no idea what a king pin was and, in any case, grease was expensive.

Another small difficulty with the car was the absence of a petrol gauge. We carried a stick, which I poked with skill into the tank, whenever the thought crossed my mind. My most dramatic 'stop' was in the centre of a four-road junction outside the old Globe Cinema in Albany Road. No-one gave a helping hand, as I pushed through the traffic, muttering unanswerable prayers. No petrol!

All the other cars in my life were to be without the hand throttle with its tightening nut in the centre of the steering wheel. Top speed was approaching twenty-five miles an hour, on a down slope and in a following wind. The roads always proved to be empty with not a car ever in front to impede my passage! That machine trundled beautifully along the highway. We called her Emma and she had been born in 1932.

So we set out on our journey to the promised land. We proudly entered the ancient village of Llandaff, up the High Street and, on the Green, parked neatly outside the Deanery.

# 14.
# MAJESTAS

Llandaff Cathedral looks back to the advent of Christianity into Britain. The faith must have found its way through the witness of Roman soldiers, many of whom married and settled in the country and it was also brought across the Channel by refugees from Gaul. However, that early Church received li.tle encouragement from outside Britain, until Constantine the First, in 313 A.D., officially allowed Christianity to be tolerated. That was when, for the first time, buildings were designed for Christians to assemble for worship.

When the Roman legions left the country in the fifth century, Wales was almost entirely Christian and when Augustine in 597 A.D. arrived formally from Rome to establish a Church system, as organised elsewhere in the Empire, he found that there was already in place a number of churches, bishops, monasteries and an establishment already paying homage to the authority of Rome.

The monastically-based missionaries had done their work well. They had travelled the countryside of Wales, and were regarded as holy men. So it was that Llandaff Cathedral was founded by Teilo, who died in 580 A.D., the building being established by the middle of the sixth century. Its history is surrounded by the turmoil of the Norman Conquest, centuries of alterations, additions and restorations, culminating with the disaster of a German aerial land mine in 1941.

The Parish of Llandaff, when I arrived in 1957, housed about seventeen thousand people and the Cathedral served them as their Parish

Church. The Curate of Llandaff was appointed to look after the Parish affairs, under the supervision of the Dean who also carried the title of Vicar. I knew the Dean well, as he had been the Warden of St. Michael's Theological College during my years there. He had instilled what theology was in me and my respect for his pastoral skills was immense.

So we arrived at the Deanery. Eryl Thomas was obviously pleased that I was interested in the vacancy and, to my surprise and great pleasure, I was appointed on the spot to be the next Curate of Llandaff. D'rene was eight months pregnant and possibly the Dean did not want to disturb her perilous condition with any delays. She was happy.

Salary was discussed and there was some haggling over the telephone with one of the church wardens, but the problem was resolved. The house in Thistle Way, just off Western Avenue, seemed excellent, but proved to be in desperate need of decoration. The wood of the banisters and staircase had been covered with emulsion paint, the kitchen was a disaster area and the back garden was out of control. Apart from these minor details, both D'rene and I were delighted to accept the appointment.

Our third child was expected at the tail end of February, so it was agreed that I would start work in Llandaff on the first day of April. If Martin were to arrive into the world on the expected date, we would have a clear month to organise the move. We trusted that All Fool's Day, 1957, would not be a bad omen!

The moment that such a decision was made, naturally coincided with switching off the work in hand. In the same way, the folk of Tremorfa begun to worry about my successor. This was understandable, but unsettling. There were a few matters to sort out before the big van arrived, not least the birth of a child. No delay was to be allowed.

On the dot of expectation, Martin announced his debut into the world; his timing was awkward. Eleven o'clock at night with two children tucked up in their beds, Martin made his move. Our good friends over the road came in to hold the fort, as we set out for the Royal Infirmary in our little car.

There was a problem. To D'rene's alarm, as she walked into the maternity ward, she was met by the staff nurse.

"Sorry, love, we're full."

"But I've been booked in for months!"

"Sorry, not a bed to spare."

"What do we do!"

"I'll telephone around."

We stood there like a couple of orphans in a storm. 'No room at the inn' might add spice to a Christmas story, but my thoughts were far from Biblical. D'rene was crying.

The whole production was to be diverted to St. David's Hospital on the other side of the city. So we wandered off into the night in our little Austin Seven. D'rene was really upset, as all the preparatory visits had been to the Royal and she knew the staff there.

The greeting at St. David's at two in the morning was not encouraging. I was getting concerned lest the birth might happen en-route and the child, ever after, would have to be called Austin. We found the ward.

"We're not here to accept the Royal's cast offs!"

The sister stood with elbows out, grim faced and not very happy. We were not amused.

As I left D'rene to face what lay ahead, in the small hours I set off across Cardiff to check on the rest of our brood. The house had been immaculate. D'rene had dusted, polished, moved the furniture, hoovered, sorted out shelves in the normal pregnancy explosion of absurdities. Jane had other ideas! That night as we had departed, she had been violently sick in her bed. Sheets, blankets, even the floor, her clothing, it was a disaster area. She must have only just missed the ceiling. As ever mother-in-law came to the rescue and Martin was born on that Saturday afternoon.

All was not well at St. David's Hospital. I was called to see the consultant. We walked down a passageway, whilst he explained to me in simple language that Martin might need special care as he was a spina bifida. As we talked, I absorbed the full implication of what I was being told.

When I saw D'rene in the ward, she told me the story. Even before the afterbirth had been removed, they had informed her that the baby was in trouble. That seemed insensitive to me. D'rene was in a state of shock. There were tears.

It was a relief when eventually they both returned home. Now we were five. The weeks were skipping along. I spent as much time as I could at the new house in Llandaff, where most evenings I worked alone into the small hours of the night with no financial or physical help. The house, of course, belonged to the Parish. Once again, as I strove away, I thought back to that cheerful 'bucket brigade' in Cwmdare. There was never to be a group like them. Time was pressing before we were to move to the next stage of our life.

We drove to Llandaff in our little box on wheels. D'rene carried Martin in her arms and also nursed the goldfish bowl between her legs. Stephen and Jane were buried somewhere on the back seat. There were to be fourteen house moves during our ministry and we always wondered at the speed with which we accomplished them. On the second day, the back lawn was cut and the car placed in the garage.

A few weeks later we almost had a divorce, when I attempted to help D'rene paper a ceiling. I walked out in disgust as the pasted monstrosity wound itself about my head. Never again was I asked to be in the same room as a strip of paper and, to my delight, D'rene proved herself to be an enthusiastic expert. She would not have discovered this excellence if I had persevered, not that I had the courage to explain that chauvinistic theory to her.

The water tank was held together by a piece of elastoplast, where on one side it was rotten with rust. I asked one of the wardens that the tank be replaced.

"Is it actually leaking?"

"The piece of plaster is doing its stuff."

"Let me know when it leaks!"

My call to the Dean produced a more reasonable response and, thereafter, all such problems became his.

At the back of my mind, I realised that working in a Cathedral was to be more demanding than any other appointment and I felt more than a little intimidated by what lay ahead. Nothing had prepared me for the large congregations and their enhanced expectations.

The first hurdle was to be the first sermon on my first Sunday. We were well into Lent and I was to perform on Passion Sunday.

I had a twelve minute slot at the morning Parish Eucharist and, as the nave was not completed, we all squeezed into the Welch Regimental Chapel. Every seat was taken, not that the numbers were great. We had no idea of the congregation explosion which was to come about when the full Cathedral was brought into use.

Nervously I did my stuff, reading every word, and was much relieved when I had finished. No-one made a single comment. Months later Charlie Chubb, who was to become a good friend, told me that he knew I was going to be fine, because I stammered and stuttered to such good effect that everyone wanted to support me. I assumed that it was meant as a compliment, as well as the truth.

The next week was memorable. The restoration after the bombing was almost completed, apart from one rather important addition. Epstein's Majestas had not arrived. The whole place was closed to the public as the final cosmetics were accomplished by a group of volunteers. There was much polishing and dusting, carrying of chairs and books and general bustle with a purpose. Then the Majestas appeared as planned.

The organ was being tuned with odd burbles and explosions of sound. Workmen scurried with intent. I sat quietly in the back row of the nave, observing all this organised frenzy. Alongside me sat Jacob Epstein. He chatted away, asking questions, rubbing his hands, rocking back and fore; it dawned upon me that this great man was nervous. I was struck dumb! What could I possibly say that might be of interest to this man! We were well matched, one a bit twitchy, the other with a stammer.

The conversation improved. He talked of the work of a Cathedral as he saw it. He asked about the people and the congregation, their ideas of artistic expression and whether they would see what he could see and understand as he understood. He was really worried about his Majestas.

As we chatted, we watched the seventeen feet of unpolished aluminium being hoisted and fixed on to the overhead drum of the Pulpitum, above the chancel steps. Epstein stopped talking. We just gazed.

For the first time I saw Christ as Epstein saw Christ. Truly it was majestic.

The face seemed to shine as it looked heavenward and away from where we sat. It was as though the Christ saw that the final journey for mankind was that we were to be 'absorbed' into the awesome presence of God. I was looking at the King of Kings going home. It was the face of the Transfiguration.

The arms hung down with the hands open towards those who dared to look. They seemed to beckon and strain to lift each one of us. These were the hands come down from the Cross to call mankind to enter the Kingdom, which Christ had made ours. Here was the strength of Christ made visible to man. Words were not needed. The invitation was not just to follow, but to be lifted up and make the journey to God, supported by the hands of Christ.

My eyes came down along the elongated robes to the hanging feet, which still carried the marks of the nails, the evidence of all the pain and suffering of mankind. I realised that the pain and suffering was also given to God.

As my eyes returned to that majestic face, I realised that I was in a place where man had come to worship for a thousand years and that this Majestas could remain there for another thousand.

By this time the organ was at full thunder and we both sat, wrapped in thought. Then, at last, he turned to me.

"Well?"

I stumbled to express my emotions. I told him what I could see. He made little comment, but seemed to listen. Later with the foolishness of youth and probably because we had sat so long together, I questioned him about the mechanics of creating such a work, and then went in feet first.

"Was it difficult for you, a practising Jew, to create a Christ for a Christian congregation?"

It was a natural question and I can recall almost his exact words.

"All my life I have searched for truth and beauty and, in the end, I discovered that it is in the idea of the Christ that they are to be found."

That was the climax of our conversation and I was never given the chance to speak to him again. As the years have passed, his words have taken on a deeper meaning. I have discussed them with many people from many nations and theologies.

Whatever your religion or lack of it, every man has to create for himself his own ideas of truth and beauty. They may not seem to be of much worth to others, but without a vision man has no place to go and life becomes just a repetitive drudge. We all need the idea of a King ... and many of us dream of His Kingdom being right here on earth.

A Cathedral is a place of prayer and one of ours was to be answered.

A few weeks into my time at Llandaff, after a morning service, a man approached me. I did not know him. He was a paediatrician at Llandough Hospital. He had heard of our worries about Martin. In no time we took him to the hospital and the polypus on the spine was found to be merely a skin growth. It was tied off and a few days later Martin was back home. It had not been a spina bifida. All was well.

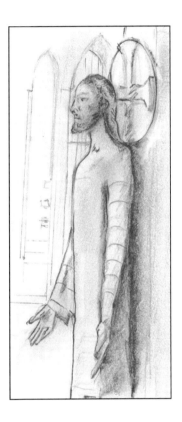

# 15.
# CHARLIE

Llandaff Cathedral was an instant tourist Mecca, if that is not a contradiction of metaphor. The Dean, the two Minor Canons and myself spent the early weeks and months giving guided tours and potted histories to the many thousands of visitors, arriving from every corner of the world. Every quarter of an hour, we climbed the pulpit, switched on the microphone and performed.

For the majority of the visitors, the main talking point was the Majestas. Some folk arrived at the West door, took one look, and dismissed what they saw as yet more modern artistic rubbish. Fortunately, the vast majority were intrigued, which enabled us to discuss what their idea of the Christ actually was. Without the normal embarrassment, I was able to talk about matters spiritual, even though we had to break through the 'Gentle Jesus, Meek and Mild' barrier. I was beginning to enjoy myself.

The formal opening of the re-built Cathedral in the presence of the Queen and the Duke of Edinburgh was all that might be expected. I could hardly believe the transformation in my life style; Tremorfa was truly another world. For a brief time we seemed to be the centre of the universe, the ecclesiastical variety. My role was insignificant, but fun.

After the pomp of that opening Service, tea was taken at the Bishop's Palace. To my surprise, Prince Philip winkled me out of a corner.

"Take me for a walk in the garden."

I really think that he wanted to escape the cup of tea ritual.

"What's a curate doing in a Cathedral?"
He had spotted my title in the Order of Service. I explained about the parish set-up. He remarked that it was refreshing to find a Cathedral with its roots firmly in the community. I could only agree with him that it was a happy marriage.

Some weeks later, Princess Margaret was in Cardiff to open the new College of Technology on Western Avenue. As her convoy passed, she spotted the spire and tower of the Cathedral and announced that there was time for a quick visit. The whole procession of vehicles was side-tracked. I chanced to be on duty and was much surprised by the sudden invasion of Special Branch, the local Police, top brass and, of course, the Royal visitor. There was no time for thought. I sent a runner to locate the Dean and gave a whirlwind performance. She obviously knew her ecclesiastical history. The boss arrived just as we finished with the entourage, to see them disappearing in a flurry of Daimlers.

Next to descend the Cathedral steps was the Prime Minister, Harold MacMillan. He was a stately figure with a face like a tired blood hound, but he was exceedingly gracious and obviously enjoyed the visit. My contribution was nil! Although I was vouchsafed a hand-shake.

That long, hot summer was a round of coaches and cars and endless visitors. There was never room to park on the Green above the Cathedral ... all the Welsh Cathedrals are in hollows! We saw all sorts and conditions of mankind, from the high to the low, all denominations and shapes and sizes. The Americans that year had 'taken us in' as part of their European tour. One American lady said it all for me.
"I like your funny accent. Say some more."
We never stopped talking.

In the middle of all this turmoil, it would have been easy to forget the real purpose of our existence and to neglect the folk in the parish. The Sunday Services were packed with locals and visitors. This enabled us to greet our own parishioners, including those who had abandoned worshipping in the Cathedral for many years. The excitement of the 'new Cathedral' was working in our favour, as people emerged out of the wilderness.

My predecessor and old friend, Edwin Davies, had conducted a Children's Service in the Lady Chapel for almost a decade with great success. Edwin had the reputation of being 'good with children'. That

Service was to be my responsibility with one major difference. It was to be held in the new nave and not in the small Lady Chapel.

My Service was scheduled to last for half an hour, squeezed in between the Parish Eucharist and Cathedral Matins. The numbers attending the Eucharist had rocketed and invariably it over-ran. My vocal congregation of youngsters gathered at the West door, raising the decibel level, as ten o'clock struck and went. At least, they did not sing, 'Why are we waiting'! Then came the charge! As one congregation fought to get out, my tiddlers ferreted their way through them, rushing in to grab the front seats. The Cathedral organist was stopped in full voluntary to be replaced by Marjorie Gibbons, who hit the keys as quickly as possible to deaden the sound. With luck, I could start the Service by ten past ten; our deadline was ten-forty as we had to evacuate our lot to make way for Cathedral Matins, which was regarded as the holiest of productions in the Cathedral life. Timing was vital.

My little darlings were there, not to raise the tone of the place, but to enjoy an act of worship. You cannot praise God with a miserable face! As we did our stuff, I was aware of the Cathedral Choir rehearsing in the basement of the Prebendal House, adding in our rare moments of silence a sense of the numinous, which I believed was not lost on those young people in the congregation. It was all part of the Cathedral atmosphere.

Most of the older worshippers in the village remembered that fearful night on the 2nd of January, 1941, when a German land mine floated on its parachute across the Parish of Llandaff, caught on the spire and exploded on the South side of the Cathedral. Ironically, on that same wartime night, another land mine demolished St. Michael's Theological College in Llandaff, but happily all the homes in the Parish were spared and no lives were lost. However, Bob White, the Cathedral Head Verger, was trapped in the wreckage and remained unconscious for three days. His recovery was miraculous.

Bob remained as Head Verger and proved to be for me an ally and a friend; yet it was many years later that I learned of that traumatic night and of his near tragedy. All that Bob reflected in his life was his great pride in what had arisen out of the ashes. He saw the children as the future and was ever willing to help me. Quickly, I had discovered a way to endear one's self to any verger. My final words in the Service were never to vary.

"Put your kneelers on the hooks. Pass all your books to the end of the aisle. End person, please take them to the back of the Cathedral and stack them neatly. Good morning, everybody. See you all next week!" That system never failed; there were no complaints from the Head Verger.

My early training in Cwmdare began to show. There I had learned that children were comfortable within set patterns; adults were no different. The Service started in the same way every Sunday. I gave the congregation a nod and off they would go.

"When I pray, I speak to God
When I listen, God speaks to me."

Then came a brief prayer for ourselves and we launched into the first hymn. It was necessary to settle them down and tune into their thoughts.

Many years later, I still find those who remind me that, not only can they repeat those opening words, but they now understand the full meaning of such a simple introduction to an act of worship. A little more listening in our lives is never wasted.

The format was the proverbial 'hymn sandwich' ... three hymns with chat in between. The chat was the problem. The first slot had to be a Jesus story to stress the impact that He made upon all those about Him. There were plenty of books with ideas and themes. This was to establish a basis of Christian teaching and was not to be a difficulty. The second slot was intended to make the teaching personal and understandable to the vast cross section of ages in front of me. Three-year olds and twelve-year olds are chalk and cheese, but as I gazed down from the pulpit, I realised that they produced another problem, because almost every child had been brought to the Cathedral by his father. Here was a congregation of men and children. The answer was to be Charlie!

Just five weeks into the problem, I told a simple story about a mouse. On the spur of the moment, I called him Charlie. The name proved to be a winner.

Charlie thought that he was a very important mouse, the most importantest mouse in the mousey world. He knew it was true because he could prove it. After all, he had jumped the highest mountain that any mouse had ever jumped. It was the hugest of jumps.

Using the microphone, I had the children pretend that they were jumping, as up and up we went and then back into our seats with a 'plonk'. Chaos reigned, but it was controlled. Everyone was smiling. Even the dads had joined in the fun!

When Charlie looked back on the mountain, he realised that it had not been much of a mountain. In fact, it was just a clump of grass. Ah well!

Then Charlie came to a large lake, as big as an ocean. You could barely see the other side. Charlie took off and leapt and leapt the biggest leap that had ever been leapt and, with a 'kerplonk', he landed on the other side. Fantastic!!! Yet when he looked back, all that it had been, if you really looked, was a puddle of murky, mucky, dirty water. His tail went down. His whiskers sank. "I'm not much of a mouse!"

Charlie made his way sadly homewards, waggleless and wobbleless, muttering as he went, "Best place is home". Into the barn he crept, where the farmer had conveniently stacked a huge mound of wheat. Charlie felt a little better, because all mice are rather fond of wheat and this pile of goodies was enough for breakfast for ever and ever and longer than that. So he sat, twiddled his whiskers and thought and scratched, as he thought, and came up with a wonderful conclusion of a thought.

"To prove that I'm the greatest mouse that ever was, I'll move this mountain of breakfast from this side of the barn to that side of the barn and that will be the finest thing that I have ever done."

He took one piece of grain, sniffed it, and toddled across the barn. He did it again and again. He began to shout, "I can do it, I can do it." Then he jumped in the air, landed upside down, waggled his feet, gyrated his tail and announced to the world, "I can do it! What a clever mouse I am, I am!"

Charlie stopped and began to think in straight lines. Of course, he could do it, but it would take a long bit of time, many months of bits of time, too many bits of time for a mouse. Charlie thought a while longer and then said in his loudest voice, which filled the barn with all his sound, "I know I can do it, but I'll be the tiredest of mouses." And the more that he thought about that, the tireder he became and, in no time at all, Charlie was fast asleep. Every person in the Cathedral made snoring noises with full crescendos, such as had never been heard in all the centuries of worship in that place.

The last two minutes of the address drove the message home. There are many hills and mountains to be conquered in our lives. Faith might be able to move mountains, but pain and suffering and ache would not go away. Jesus, like Charlie, knew that we can only tackle today what we can manage today. You must do today exactly what you can achieve today. I began to refer thereafter to the 'sacrament of the present moment'. If you do nothing, the mountain can get bigger.

That was the first story about Charlie the Mouse. Next week, I tried a tale about Archie the Spider, which really was all about Job and the art of perseverance. Then came Priscilla the Cat, who went up to London to see the Queen, but only saw a mouse because we tend to see only what we wish to see in life. God is always with us, but we tend only to see our little world and can so easily miss Him. Our vision can be so limited that we can end up with tunnel vision and echo the Psalmist's description of the stupidity of man, 'The fool hath said in his heart, There is no God!' Teen-agers have a remarkable ability to reach this conclusion.

I only became aware of the impact of Charlie the Mouse when a small child dragged her father up to me at the end of that Service and, with all the wonder of toddledom, posed a question.

"Was it Charlie the Mouse that the cat saw under the Queen's chair?" With no hesitation, I replied, "Come next week and we'll have a peep together."

That father looked at me with half a smile.

"See you next week, Bob."

That was when I realised that a child had remembered a story that was three weeks old and was interested in a character, which I should not abandon. Charlie had to be resurrected!

Whit Sunday was upon us, the birthday of the Church, when we think about the Holy Spirit being alive in each person. I wanted to talk about that first Christian experience of 'new life' in the way that the Bible had painted it, but was not certain that it would convey the idea of God, as I thought of Him. Charlie came to the rescue.

Charlie was back home after his holiday in London, where you remember he had found himself being chased by a cat in Buckingham Palace, although that was a story for another day. Charlie wandered through the farmhouse. He came across a wooden leg and promptly went up it. There he discovered a whole new world, which he could not understand. After all, he was only a small mouse. Charlie was surrounded by masses of wires, some thin and some thick, and they were all vibrating and creating tremendous noises. This was very strange. He had never seen such a peculiar sight in all his mouse years. Further along were lines of little hammers. Up and down they went, banging away at the wires. This was enormous fun, but very, very strange. Then Charlie bent down, waggled his whiskers out of the way, and peeped through a crack in the wood. What a peculiar sight! Now he saw strips of black and white things all bobbing up and down. This was a bit of a puzzle and he had no idea where he was or what it was.

By this time hands were popping up in the Cathedral, as the children were dying to reveal how perceptive they were. Soon, enough hands were raised for me to ask the question.

"Where is Charlie?"

"Inside a piano!"

Everyone smiled. Some dads had whispered the answer, as on I went.

Charlie shut one eye ... so did the congregation ...he squeezed a bit lower and saw fingers waggling ... we were all waggling away ... and they were attached to two hands. The congregation sat up straight. At last, Charlie understood.

There was, of course, no way in which he could call it a piano, but whatever it was named, he had found a human being behind all those bits of machinery and those remarkable sounds. This was a great discovery for a mouse. Behind the wires and the hammers and the keys was the farmer's wife and she loved music.

We had all enjoyed the nonsense of seeing a piano through the eyes of a mouse. The last minutes were spent explaining that behind my hands and feet and eyes and all of me, there is a God who loves me ... and that bit of God we have called the 'Holy Spirit'. The Holy Spirit is the little bit of God inside me.

On the spur of the moment, I asked the children to use actions to fit the words. 'The Holy Spirit is the little bit of God' ... we all pointed to the heavens ... 'inside me' ... we then dug our fingers into our ribs to show that God was right inside each one of us.

This was another lesson learned by me. Thereafter, all the sessions were to end with a catch phrase and a punch-line ... and matched by actions. The Cathedral was to be filled with madly waving arms and roof shattering incantations. It proved to be a great way to end every address. Everyone was awake!

The on-going saga of Charlie was to last for all my years in Llandaff. Around that mouse, a whole life style evolved. He always awoke at seven in the morning in every story that I told and the children, with no prompting, called out the chimes on the Church clock in the village where Charlie lived. People came to have breakfast with him and that was often the opening for the next big adventure. His best friend was Freddie the Field Mouse. Breakfast was always described in sordid details, bringing groans of disbelief from the children, even though their imaginations were well ahead of mine

For a number of weeks, Charlie went to School and became addicted to arithmetic. He could only understand the simplest of sums and often the youngsters had to help him. The hidden meaning behind the stories was also simple and hopefully understood by the youngest in the congregation.

Yourself plus another can do oodles, but yourself plus oodles of others can perform miracles. Children can understand that.

Yourself minus your faults and your failings and your feebleness equals growth. That is common sense to anyone ... even grown-ups might grasp the point!

All good things divided equals good things for all. That was simple. The Gospel story about the loaves and the fishes fitted that thought nicely.

Good mathematics equalled Christianity in action. When I met the young people in the street, I was asked whether I was having a plus or a minus day and we all knew that to put it right all that I needed was addition or subtraction. Their young minds could nimble their way through any situation, if given the chance.

The ignorant passer-by must have wondered when a child across the road from me would grab an imaginary Church bell rope and start pulling ... and I would do the same! No words needed to be spoken, as we both understood that it was Charlie the Mouse's language for, 'I must go to Church'. That was the message of the church bell, as explained by

Charlie. We reached the point in the Services when I would do the actions and they would call out the words. Even more fun was to do the actions together and say the words silently in your mind. That produced a lovely atmosphere, as in complete silence four hundred of us waved our arms about with broad grins on our faces. It was as though we all belonged to a secret society. I suppose we did.

We took Charlie away on holiday and discovered how mice survived in other parts of the world. We even learned the Highway Code from Charlie. It was, of course, a Highway Code with a 'heavenly' meaning. I quietly wondered what impact we made on the future drivers in Llandaff. The microphone enabled me to use a helicopter with all the appropriate sound effects. Concorde would have speeded things up, but we were still able to whiz around the world in our imaginations to discover that Charlie had mouse connections in every nook and granary. After all, the whole world belongs to God and we all belong to each other. And, naturally, Charlie the Mouse was colour blind!

One Christmas, we had a painting competition. A large drawing of Charlie outside Llandaff Cathedral was produced and given to each child to colour. Over forty years later my daughter, Jane, still has her contribution beautifully framed and proudly on view. Ever since those days, Christmas cards still arrive with a mouse somewhere on the front and an extra greeting for Charlie the Mouse on the inside.

It quietly dawned upon me that one of the attractions of Charlie was not the detail of the week's story, but the expectation of what was to happen the following week. It was important that the listeners always felt that Charlie had never quite grasped the situation that had befallen him, but that they had and wanted to help him. They had to be involved. As often as possible, Charlie was left hanging by the smallest toe nail on his left foot, preferably on the extreme edge of a precipice, with positively no means of escape. We all knew that Charlie would find a solution to his calamity ... next week!

Children were playing a larger and larger part in my ministry. The two Minor Canons and myself were welcomed at the Church Primary School, where we took the opening morning lessons. I never used Charlie in my talks, although the class often brought him into the discussions. I did not realise that all this work with the young would eventually lead me to Liverpool, but all that was a long way ahead.

In an attempt to introduce the school children to the Cathedral, I decided that there should be a Challenge Week. There were many options. The aim was to hold a half hour session after school. The carrot I used was a programme, which was called Express Adventure. Mary and John were to set out to a city called Do-as-you-Please.

The story started in a tunnel, which twisted the wrong way. It was a convoluted story! The youngsters came out of loyalty, but as the week wore on I became as bored as they were. It was an exercise never to be repeated.

Sunday Schools were still very popular. Nominally I was in charge, but the teachers were well capable of handling their own programme and all that they needed from me was encouragement. I did introduce a system of coloured cards and stars with a more structured syllabus. In my heart, I knew that I was just interfering.

That left me with Charlie the Mouse, who was to thrive and survive. His followers never wavered. Each episode was tried out on D'rene late every Saturday night and she provided all the encouragement that I needed. Then with my brain still in overdrive, she went to sleep.

# 16.
# WORK IS PLAY

Discipline and discipleship add up to about the same principle. The one requires the other and cannot stand alone. We read of our spiritual betters, who have gone before us, being able to survive on as little as four hours sleep each day. In my tiny mind I wonder how much more saintly they might have been, if they had received their statutory eight, tucked up in their little cots with no central heating and stone-slabbed floors. It might even have done wonders for their tempers! But such thoughts about eight hours of sleep were really academic; I failed to reach the magic number.

We certainly had bred the most charming, disciplined and well-tempered off-spring. However, even such paragons made the odd demands in the small hours. My theory was that the moment that I left the house at six-forty each morning, they would all fall into the deepest of slumbers and then awake at a more acceptable time.

When I returned to the fold at eight-thirty, there they all were, fed, watered, dusted and dressed. D'rene in common with most females had performed yet another miracle. To this day, I cannot recall ever having the doubtful privilege of changing a nappy. Those were the days of outdoor lines and Persil washing whiter. All this I was spared.

We clergy appeared for Matins at seven and it was regarded as unspiritual not to be on your knees at least ten minutes before kick-off. Matins having been negotiated, there was a slight lull in the activity until the duty priest appeared, fully robed, preceded by a server and heading for the appropriate altar. Each morning we then shared in a Communion Service. At the tail end, we all spent at least a quarter of an hour in private meditation. In the winter, we were enveloped in large, black, clerical cloaks, impervious to all ecclesiastical draughts. We were a wondrous medieval sight as we walked the streets of Llandaff, adding a bit of tone for any tourist chancing upon us.

The whole game-plan was repeated each evening. We processed, fully robed, behind the Cathedral choir for Choral Evensong at six sharp. I was lucky to be home by seven and thus missed the bath tub and talcum powder battle. I arrived in time to kiss "goodnight" to the three sweetest-smelling children in South Wales ... Stephen with his nose in a book, Jane looking for trouble and Martin fast asleep. There was just enough space for a pause before setting out for the evening activity.

As with most people, my life became a set routine. It meant that D'rene was receiving little support in the home and I wonder who and what is neglected these days when over forty-five per cent of the work force is female. That must put immense pressures on the marriages. Although I had little time to call my own, I was very happy in the Parish. As much time as possible was spent on house calls. Each visit created the need for further calls and the days were not long enough.

One experiment was to visit every home in two of the longest streets in the Parish, even calling back at night to make certain that I met every person. In such a large Parish, it was impossible to see at home everyone who came to the Cathedral, with the result that some never received a call, even though there were four staff members. This was a fact of life, only matched by the thought that most people must have wondered what we clergy did all day, as they never saw us. My intensive visiting ... each call could last at least half an hour ... produced baptisms, the need for further sick visits, home communions and, in one particular house, the need for urgent financial assistance.

The end result of the experiment was that other areas were neglected. Assessing priorities and the wise use of time proved to be a sophisticated way of selecting those who were to be ignored.

If there had been no discipline over the time set aside for prayer, that would have been the first to suffer. I had been taught that the primary purpose for the existence of a priest was "to offer his people to God".

A failure to do just that would have made a nonsense of all our flurry of activity. The priest is not a social worker or a psychiatrist. He exists to bring God into the lives of people, in reality to show them that God is already with them! Many years later, I found myself attending "Work Study Seminars" when young priests spent much time discussing the "theology of work" and the "role of the priesthood". Our old-fashioned input was ignored, but we could smile when our "old ideas" were wrapped in a new jargon, as the young men set themselves up as trend setters. Maybe we had appeared the same to our elders!

The large numbers attending the Cathedral tended to remove our feelings of guilt and failure over home visiting. Up to this stage in my ministry I had concentrated much energy in producing what we called "pew fodder", as the size of your congregation seemed to be a barometer of success. In the Parish of Llandaff the pews were full! This left the question as to what we actually thought we were doing as we called in the homes of our parishioners. There are too many tales of the result of straightforward Bible bashing and shiny-faced evangelical zeal and the inevitable backlash.

There was the tale of Father Smith, the Vicar of Rumney in Cardiff. He was a powerful, straight spoken, high-church character, a useful source of anecdotes. He told one tale against himself. During a round of house calls, he knocked at a particular door. It was opened by a middle-aged lady with her curlers on top. Father Smith gave the opening salvo.

"You are one of my sinners in this parish."

He said that she didn't even blink, hoisted up her bosom and saw him off.

"You are the other one!"

The door slammed.

I had long discovered that it was foolish to arrive at a home with pre-conceived ideas of the needs of the people. That approach also assumed that you have answers to their problems. The common-sense attitude boiled down to rather a simple question, "How are you?" Most folk are delighted to be asked; the difficult part is listening to the real content of the answer.

The surprise in Llandaff, after my experiences in Tremorfa, was the warmth of the welcome, as it suggested that there really was a need for me to visit ... not that it was always evident on the first call. My ultimate conclusion was that no-one ever really listens to anyone and that the parson is at his best in his job when he sits down, has yet another cup of tea and enjoys the chat. I was sure that this was right, as long as the eventual outcome of all this nebulous activity was offered to God. This was part of the discipline of discipleship. The daily round continued.

The Cathedral was to offer much more. Naturally it played a significant part in the life of the Diocese, hosting large Services to mark the overall activity of the Deaneries. There seemed to be an endless procession of ladies under large hats carrying banners up the main aisle to the High Altar, where we clergy rescued them and with the utmost care balanced the banners against the nearest pillar, leaving the ladies to wander off in search of their seats. Battle was then rejoined at the end of the Service, when they shuffled back to reclaim their individual banners. There was always a problem. It was impossible to return the right banner to the right person.

"That's not mine."

"It doesn't matter."

"Mine's Abercwmboi."

"Take it!"

Some remained kneeling, like beached whales, with a pleading look on their faces.

"Get up now!"

Speed was essential because the redistribution had to be completed within the length of a hymn. The only rule was: "Don't give a Guide banner to a Scout!"

That first summer in Llandaff I attended the Annual Fete, but played little part in it. Perhaps that was the way that I should have left it, but at the turn of the year, I formed a committee. The intention was to breathe new life into the Llandaff Annual Summer Fete.

We had an abundance of talent, all matched with enthusiasm. The first important task was to discover who had done what in the past. No-one was to be overlooked, only encouraged for further endeavour. Above all, the Mothers' Union Strawberry Tea Marquee was not to be disturbed. My contribution was, apparently, to pray for an abundant fruit season and offer no advice to the Mothers' Union. Mrs. Rose Jenkins, Pontcanna, had been in charge for many a year and had achieved perfection. That left everything else for us to organise.

We planned for a Holiday Fun Week to climax with the Summer Fete on Llandaff Fields. During that week, the Cathedral bell ringers, with the tireless Nevil James in charge, took over the Green in the village with a stall surrounded by gas bottles, posters and balloons. For a shilling a time, you sent your balloon on its journey. The eventual winner was to end up (or is it down?) in Central Europe to win a princely twenty-five pounds. Every passing customer was urged to bring the family to the Saturday Fete. Of course, there were complaints. The more straight-laced felt that we were lowering the tone of Llandaff. We merely murmured that each balloon was sent heavenwards with a prayer. The fact that the prayer was that it might reach Russia or further was not mentioned. We all enjoyed ourselves.

Jim Armitage was appointed the secretary and proved to be an inspired choice. As the weeks rolled on before the event, Jim and his wife, Doris, appeared almost nightly in our home in Thistle Way to plot and plan into the small hours. At least, Jim and D'rene did most of the scheming, whilst Doris and I dozed quietly in our chairs. But I am certain that the Push Football Competition was my stupid idea and I clearly can recall where that idea had originated.

I remembered the long, hot, sunny summers of my childhood in Llanharan in the Vale of Glamorgan, when the country's unemployment level topped two and a quarter million, almost all men. The local colliery hooter would sound at four in the afternoon, most days, to indicate that there would be no work the next day. The unemployed miners sat on their haunches on the pavement outside Bert Beard's the Blacksmith with Woodbines, unlit, and no hope. Horses still came to be shod and we young lads were sometimes allowed to pump the bellows as the anvil rang with hammer blows at the rate of two on the anvil and one on the horse-shoe. The rhythm was hypnotic; we breathed in the blue air with the scent of burning hoof. For a young lad it was a magic place and we barely saw the tragic huddles of men with their grey faces, wrapped in mufflers and caps. Llanharan never recovered from those years of depression; yet all my memories are of fun in childhood.

Each Friday night, I joined the stampede as we ran down the road to the local cinema with three-pence in our sticky hands. That unbelievable sum of money was only ever given at the last minute, after we had been angels all day long and had helped mother with the Friday evening chore of cleaning all the kitchen brass. We never knew until ten to seven how angelic we had actually been. I was always open to bribery, if at the end there was a chance to see Flash Gordon!

Saturdays started badly in our home. Each of those mornings we were faced with senna tea; we were brought up in the era of "open bowels are next to Godliness". Senna tea was appalling, but it did mean that the day could only improve. The more wealthy families graduated to California Syrup of Figs. Eventually that elixir arrived on our menu and I loved it so much that I drank it like pop. I cannot recall any disastrous consequences. Others had to endure Castorette Tablets, which D'rene assures me she was able to palm and dispose of with magical skill. When you consider the constant attack on our young bowels, we should have been nearer God than we were. Yet, as a child, Saturday was a tremendous day because of all the happenings on the village Recreation Field.

Rarely was I allowed to visit the Field, but the top of our garden overlooked the main railway line from London to Fishguard and on the other side of that line was the Playing Field. I had a grandstand view over all the activities. I sat and gazed.

In winter there was rugby. Even in the Junior School we were taught the basics of the game, once each week in rain, wind and snow. Everyone played. Our school had no rugby kit; so we dressed as best we could in old clothes and hoped that we knew who was on our side. Many a hand-off on my cold nose convinced me that I would never play for Wales.

In summer we played cricket and the village had a great team. There were bowling greens and a fine pavilion, alongside of which were three hard tennis courts and one rather bumpy grass one. As we grew older, all this gave us great joy as we competed together and began to notice that girls were not so stupid after all. However, my biggest memory must be the wonderful Summer Fetes in Llanharan.

Folk came from neighbouring villages in great numbers. It was the purple period for the Jazz Bands and I can still hear the drone of bazookas, humming the pop tunes of the day and glimpse, out of the past, the twirling capes, coloured hats and high stepping legs of the dreaming adolescents. We shouted our encouragement at the slow bicycle races; some riders were able to balance motionless for an eternity of minutes. We urged at full breath our local tug-o-war team, as the men struggled to out-pull Pencoed and Brynna and Pontyclun and Llantrisant and anyone who fancied their chances. There were races for all age groups and I was so proud when my dad won the over-fifties sprint, with trousers tucked into his woollen stockings and sleeves rolled up. I suspected that the potential village villains all noted that Sergeant Evans could outrun them. Sack races followed three-legged races and the egg and spoon tumbles brought as much joy as the contortions of the obstacle race combatants. It was a form of inter-village war with a certain amount of blood-letting.

The finale was always the Fancy Dress Parade and we, the timid ones, envied all the glamour of the brave. Llanharan Prize Silver Band provided the culture. Their practice night was on a Friday in the band shed and when I was a small child, I went to sleep as, just across the railway lines, there thumped a remarkable rendering of Orpheus in the Underworld, played rather slowly with more of a beat than a tune. I knew no better; so it was the best.

But for me, on those wonder days, the high spot was always the Push Football Competition. All of this was etched into my soul and, at last, in Llandaff I was to be given a chance to relive my wide-eyed, childhood dreams.

Push Football was to be the main event of the rejuvenated Llandaff Summer Fete. The national rugby hero of the day was that elusive wizard of the side step, Cliff Morgan. We could hardly believe our good fortune when he agreed to help, organising teams from Cardiff, Newport and other local sides. This was good stuff. Fever was high and contagious. Even the Llandaff Mothers' Union decided to field a team, formidable enough to send a tremor into the hearts of mere men. The Young Wives added glamour, but no weight! In the Parish lived an international referee, who willingly, in ignorance, offered to blow his whistle.

On the Wednesday, a large package arrived at our house. It was the ball, squared off and flat. Friday night we took the box up to the Green for the "public blowing up" of the ball. The bell ringers proved their worth. We pumped for a very long time and people stayed to discuss the size of it and to give it the odd prod.

"Just a bit more wind, boys!"

"This is no job for a woman. Stand back!"

"Who are you calling a woman?"

"Just a bit more wind!"

At last, there it stood, waiting for the morrow. Red and yellow and blue and about four foot high ... we could hardly wait!

The day promised well with a dawn full of sunshine and the bluest of skies. In good time the stalls were manned and even the grass looked polished in readiness. The Nautical Cadets from the Reardon Smith Sea Training School had ship-shaped a Bosun's Chair and were busily testing the rigging.

"Mary had a little lamb ... one, two, three, four".

The amplifiers were working. We were ready. The gates were opened and the customers poured in by the hundred. I was relieved that it had been a good strawberry season.

Jack Evans, our international referee, blew his whistle to start the first game of Push Football. The opposing sides had lined up on their twenty-five yard lines. Both teams set off at the first blast and charged together. They were well matched and arrived at the ball at precisely the same time. There was a mighty explosion! The poor ball disintegrated and allowed both teams to meet, head-on, at a rate of knots. There was a tangled mass of arms and legs and a modicum of unecclesiastical language. Then we all fell apart in roars of laughter. That was the end of Llandaff's Push Football bonanza and my dreams.

However, all was not lost. A seven-aside rugby match was promptly organised. The rules were gentlemanly adapted for the ladies for them to play touch football. Those females did extremely well. The men were systematically flattened the moment that they touched the ball. The Mothers' Union gave no quarter. The Young Wives were in a pulverising mood. The crowds thoroughly enjoyed it. One veteran Cardiff forward was heard to mutter as four ladies sat on him.

"They're tougher than the Pontypool front row!"

The referee was redundant and wisely biased in favour of the so-called weaker sex. I cannot recall who won what, but in the end that was not important.

Other Carnivals were to follow in later years, but not one of them reached such a climax before it had hardly started. I never again suggested that we hire a ball and happily pushed the whole episode into my folk memory.

There was another experiment which rather went over the top. With all the youngsters on holiday in the Parish, I decided that each one of them probably had a pet at home. In a weak moment, I decided that the long summer vacation would be lightened if we organised a Pet Show. Ideas tumbled in with great enthusiasm. About one thing I was determined; there were to be no losers.

I knew that each child thought that his own pampered and over-fed monster was the best in the world. It took much cunning to devise categories which might embrace all shapes and sizes and absurdities. I suppose that I should not have been surprised that not one village vet was prepared to come within a mile of the event, but I was able to extract many prizes from them. The Show was to be held in the Church Memorial Hall. The selection panel in the end was comprised of grand-mothers, who were wise to the wiles of the young, old enough to be beyond bribery or to be intimidated by anyone. The shop-keepers were given no choice but to provide prizes; I agreed not to reveal their names. I began to suspect the wisdom of my enthusiasm!

Happily the day was fine enough for the event to be held in the open air on the Memorial Hall car park. The contestants could be well separated. The need for that had not occurred to me!

It was not easy to decide on the longest or shortest or twistiest tail. Then there was the best smile, the most understanding eyes, the cuddliest and the friendliest. Grass snakes vied with hamsters and I kept an eye open lest there might have been a python.

I realised that we had got away with the biggest con-trick of that summer holiday. I had discovered that it was possible to skate on thin ice, even when the temperature was in the middle seventies. We never attempted it again. Llandaff appeared to be relieved.

It seemed important to me that we should create opportunities for the parishioners to meet outside the normal round of worship. This led us to hold a Parish Dance on a grand scale. The only venue had to be Bindles. This was the popular dance hall on the edge of the sea at Cold Knap in Barry, which was about ten miles away. Yet again there was total enthusiasm with no difficulty in selling some three hundred tickets.

The Bindles management really organised the evening together with the food. Our input would be small. Of course, we had to work hard to produce a large Tombola Stall, which ensured the financial success of the evening. I did the rounds of the main breweries in Cardiff. Their form of morning coffee put a smile on my face and the result was we could also have a monster Prize Draw. The Dean had been the Vicar of Risca many years before and suggested that we use the Steve Beaumont Dance Band, which originated from that parish. They were fantastic, ideal for the fifties style of music and dancing. I was to be surprised when Steve sent us a travelling clock as a "thank you" present when we eventually left Llandaff. We were to use Steve a number of times during our sojourn in the Parish.

On that first night, it all went with a swing. Even the net of balloons worked to order. It had taken us three hours to blow them up in the afternoon. The Prize Draw was to be handled by a female journalist from the Western Mail. I heard myself announce that the draw was about to commence and that our celebrity was well known to everyone. The Dean had organised her to ensure publicity. Sadly, we did not take the Western Mail and I had stupidly not written her name down. To cover my confusion I threw in the remark, "All you may know her, but I've no idea who she is!" This was greeted with a laugh, but she was not fooled and thankfully whispered her name. I was not much of a compere.

Another winning piece of parish activity emerged from a chat with John Gould. Together we dreamt up a Parish Music Hall. The ingredients were simple. Each and every organisation was to be given a spot in the programme. The show was to last for three hours and we packed the Memorial Hall for four nights with no difficulty.

The cast was so large that they all had to assemble in the open air on the car park and were in strict order dragged on to the stage, performed, and then speedily ejected out of the other side of the hall. My task was to fill in with anecdotes for the time it required for the battles to be won backstage. Too often I was told in a stage whisper ... "Keep going!" Once they had performed, they dashed around to the back of the hall, where by the end of the evening they were packed in like sardines. It was a great success.

Motor car treasure hunts were the in-thing in those days; so we obviously had to organise one for the Parish. The Vale of Glamorgan is full of tiny hamlets, ancient pubs, old stone churches, castles and all the historical bric-a-brac of yesteryear. It was tailor-made for a treasure hunt. A route was fixed. Photographs of landmarks were produced. Verbal teasers had been tortured on to paper. The preparation was completed ... almost!

The evening before the big event, Seward Ashcroft took me as navigator for the final check on the feasibility of our clues. We set out at ten o'clock at night. I was quickly to discover that Seward was a Welsh Rally driver. I should have been warned! We hurtled through the narrow lanes with a slamming of brakes and a screech of tyres. I was too young to die! At midnight, I peeped through the letter box and D'rene said that even in the gloom I was green around the gills. I declared the course driveable. The following evening went without mishap and was rounded off with grub and ale in a country pub.

The work in Llandaff seemed to be going with a swing and it was a joy to see smiling faces in the pews and to be greeted across the street as a friend. This surely was the way that a Parish should respond ... as a family and that was what we were.

# 17.
# QUESTIONS

The longer that I stayed in Llandaff, the larger was the impact of Charlie the Mouse upon my life. I was asked to visit other churches to speak to groups of youngsters and they always expected a Charlie story, not always the easiest of requests as it takes time to build up a character in someone's mind. Sunday School Deanery Associations began to call on me as though I was some kind of expert. One episode found its way on to steam radio in a Service for Children. There were requests for magazine articles. I felt that I was becoming a bit of a Charlie! Fortunately, my daily round was about other things.

The younger clergy of those days had been given little training in preparation for visiting hospitals. Hospitals can be intimidating places. Doctors and nurses surrounded themselves in an alien world to such an extent that they could barely be seen as normal human beings. They fostered the mystery of their discipline, which resulted in such awe from the rest of us mortals that, as a mere curate, I felt totally inadequate.

Ten years later, I was to be the secretary for the Liverpool Diocesan Hospital Chaplains and was called upon to organise, with little help at that time from the Training Department, two or three study days each year and did so for twelve years. Eventually, the training of Chaplains was accepted by the Health Authority as part of its responsibility. All of this was a long way ahead and in Llandaff we all had to learn the hard way ... at the expense of the patients!

Rookwood Hospital was under the pastoral care of the Cathedral clergy. I was given two wards and there I cut my teeth on the bed-bound victims. Little did I realise that it was the patients who were intimidated by the appearance of the dog-collar and they were firmly trapped with no escape from my stuttering advances.

One of my wards was for paraplegics, who lived there for weeks and months and years. Quickly I discovered that platitudes were of no value. These men were cynically inured against the casual enquiry about their health or the calorific content of their food and had no interest in throw-away remarks concerning the average rainfall in Llandaff. There was no way I could ask whether they were getting better or how long they were expecting to stay in hospital or even offer any sunny words about the future.

The initial task for me was to be accepted as a human being and to win their confidence. I learnt quickly that, once I relaxed, the medical team was superb and we were on the same side. The cleaning ladies, paper-men, nurses and doctors, they were a real team. I was recognised as a legitimate member of the hospital family with my specific contribution to make ... I was expected to make it and that should not have surprised me!

The real breakthrough for me came when Ronnie, aged fifteen, arrived on the ward. Chubby, round-faced, full of smiles, Ronnie was suffering from muscular dystrophy and was going to die. He knew that he was going to die. That information was also immediately known by every other patient on the ward. There was no way in which the fact could be avoided or softened, because Ronnie was aware that we all knew what was ahead of him. This was tough.

We all instinctively loved Ronnie and our love was more than pity. Pity was of no value to him. It would only create a barrier, which would have left him lonely and isolated from the rest of the ward. Each one of us had to remove that barrier. It was not easy.

The ward was just a war-time hut with brown polished lino, cream walls, open wooden beams and fifteen beds on either side, each with its little wooden cupboard to hold a man's possessions. There was a bare table with wooden chairs, no radio and, of course, no television. It was not much of a place in which to die!

Ronnie could hardly move as he lay on his bed. His first request on every visit was for a scratch. Even that was beyond his strength. You cannot deal with an itch without becoming a friend and I must have been a good scratcher!

One day, when I was helping him and his head was turned away from me, Ronnie asked his question.

"Bob, what is the point of my life?"

There had to be an answer.

This was the cry of mankind from the beginning of time. Libraries have been filled, the world over, in an attempt to give an answer. I could not walk away from the question

With hindsight, I believe that my response took many visits and, in the end, was not good enough for a fifteen-year old lad whose life had barely begun. Ronnie was to die a few weeks later. His parents lived in Birkenhead and were to send me a Parker pen in thanking me for the friendship which I had given their son. Perhaps, friendship had been all that was required, yet, at that time, words had been necessary.

To say to a young man that his body was not really the most important part of his being would have sounded trite and insulting to his zest for life. Ronnie was never to climb Snowdon, run a half marathon, make love or realise any ambition. Yet he was alive and I could not write him out of the script as one of life's losers. In my language, I felt that Ronnie could bring to God a complete being, even though he was wasting away on a hospital bed. At every stage in our lives, there is a God-given level of completeness, which is our attainable state of perfection. In this way, a two-year old child can be as perfect as a twenty-year old man. In that sense, Ronnie could reach a state of life, not only acceptable to God, but strong enough for God to shine through and touch all those about him. God could use Ronnie.

The body can be a drag, even for the healthiest of persons. We can easily accept that an eighty-year old can state that she is tired of her body and would be glad when it was done with for good. Ronnie had reached that stage at the age of fifteen and was not less a person because of it. However, I was not certain that Ronnie could actually accept the fact at his age that his body was a burden. I was wrong. Ronnie was always to be ahead of me.

It was equally difficult to point out to Ronnie that his life was a remarkable example to others. Yet, that was the truth. When he arrived in the ward, every other patient had stopped grumbling. Ronnie might have been approaching death; nevertheless, he retained an enthusiasm and bubble for life which made all those about him examine their futures and attitudes. His presence had utterly changed that ward! Ronnie had not only shown others how to get the most out of life, he had passed that gift on to them. His strength was shared by the weakest and marvelled at by the strongest. The small world of that ward had been changed for good. Ronnie had done that. Yet, in no way was he aware of what he had achieved; that knowledge might have given him little consolation.

Another avenue of thought was that we are but pilgrims on this earth and a complete life can only be found in union with God. I knew what words I might use; the full implication of them was beyond me! So I spoke the thought aloud and to my surprise, it was on this level of discussion where Ronnie and I were able to explore and communicate. I believe that Ronnie not only understood the idea of union with God, but was well beyond my fumbling thoughts. I should not have been surprised, nor should I have underestimated him. His search for God was concentrated and urgent. Time was not on his side.

Ronnie must often have been awake into the small and difficult hours of the night with nothing but his mind in overdrive. I discovered that the easiest path for me was to chat about the life of Jesus, making the story as real and alive as I could, and then stand back to see where it took our minds.

The Gospel story is not only ideal for meditation with neatly arranged passages ending in enigmatic punch lines, it also happens to be an interesting narrative about a man who turned the world upside down. Ronnie was always ahead of me, asking probing questions and finding his own answers. Looking at Jesus in this way is merely examining the portrait of God clearly expressed in a human life.

As we looked for the human face of Jesus, it became obvious that the driving force behind the human facade was God. Here was the major clue to life. It was but a small step to open our eyes, look about us, and see that God was at work through each of us. This simplicity was staggering. Ronnie worked it out and I trailed behind him.

The evening paper-man would be saying the right thing at the right time to a patient, because God could only use that paper-man at that time and place. This was God at work in man! The wonder of it was that the paper-man would not realise that God was at work in him. Ronnie was seeing people in a different way. Ronnie took the thought even further.

This surely was the way in which Jesus saw mankind. Here was the answer to the question ... "What is the point of my life?" Our lives are not our own to live as we wish ... sin is thinking otherwise ... because at all times we belong to God. The point of my life is that I must learn to open it to God.

Sadly, we are all too busy trying to control our own destinies. This blur of activity conceals the hand of God from us to such an extent that we finally believe that we can control our own lives. Some of us think that we are very important, even indispensable. Ronnie was way past all this. He had answered his own question about the purpose of life. God had responded to his problem. This is God's creation and Ronnie knew that he was part of it.

In later years, many folk were to ask about the purpose of life. In answer, I would chat about Ronnie whose dilemma was far greater and more urgent than that of most people. Our pin-pricks turn to dust in comparison. Ronnie has helped many to put their little worlds into perspective.

The basic answer had appeared to be so simple. "It is not your life. You belong to God." Of course, if you actually believe that you are in charge of your own life, you will eventually be left with the question ... "What's the point of all this?" We are meant to live for God. At first, I found that hard to understand, but life changed for Ronnie when he understood, even though he still had to face the pain and agony of living and dying.

Then, there was Ann. Ann was never able to ask me the question. She was nearly seventeen, rather pretty, rather shy and totally unsure of the world about her. I thought that she was just a normal member of the Youth Club. In the crowd, she tried to merge into the background, hoping to be overlooked, yet wishing to be noticed. Ann was still in her awkward age. Of all those young people, I shall never forget her.

A telephone call to the house in Thistle Way sent me in haste to the Cardiff Royal Infirmary. The news appalled me. There I found Ann, deeply unconscious, in the Intensive Care Unit. Two days later she was dead.

It was to be a long forty-eight hours during which the care of her parents and the unanswered questions were to be in my uppermost thoughts. Ann was only a child, deeply loved by her mother and father, for whom she was the centre of the universe. They were never to understand what happened to their daughter.

Yet again, I was to find that words about the love of God were useless. I could only show my love towards them. Hindsight told me that God is quite capable of showing His love when we just hold hands. When the words begin to sound like theological clap-trap, it is better to hold a hand and keep quiet.

Ann worked in an office in the city. There she had fallen in love with the intensity of a teen-ager, but her world had collapsed when the imagined affair came to an abrupt end. She was devastated and could not cope.

That evening, when her parents returned home after a visit to the cinema, as they opened the front door there was a smell of gas. Ann was in the kitchen. Rushed to hospital, she never spoke again. Mother and father were defeated. Not one of us had sensed the trauma which had led to the tragedy. Nothing had warned us of the possibility of suicide.

The medical team knew almost immediately that Ann would not recover. The brain scan was flat with no sign of activity. Three times in twenty-four hours the readings were checked. The conclusion was obvious. Ann's brain was clinically dead. To us at her bedside there seemed to be life. Her hands were warm, her cheeks were red and with the aid of a machine her breathing was regular. It was hard to accept that she was dead.

The consultant indicated that we had come to the end and that Ann could not be sustained on the machines. This was hard to accept. and I became party to the discussion. I was left wondering at the courage of that mother and father as they clung to each other and I silently applauded the dignity of their ultimate sense of purpose when they finally agreed. The decision seemed to give them strength and they lifted their heads.

We stayed together most of the night and the hours stretched into eternity. Mainly we talked about Ann with all the questions out in the open. They felt guilt and their remorse tore them apart. All I knew was that as the night passed, they survived with a deeper knowledge of themselves and had begun to live with those unanswered questions.

Dawn was breaking as we left the hospital. The ward sister came out with us into the morning light. When at last we both returned to the Unit, she broke down and cried. All that I could do was to put my arms about her and share the grief. There were no words. Someone had to care for the carers and I reckoned that I had carried a fair share of that.

Days later came the final hurdle. At the Service in the Cathedral, I read the famous passage in 1 Corinthians 13, the great hymn of love. Possibly it was rejection in love which had proved too much for Ann and had decided her to choose death. In the darkness of her sense of rejection, she had lost sight of all the other love with which her family and friends had surrounded her. At the end, all that was possible for us to do was to surround her again with love.

"There is nothing love cannot face. There is no limit to its faith, its hope and its endurance. Love will never come to an end."

Somewhere in those words I found the answer to all the pain and suffering of mankind ... and to all of man's questions. There really is nothing that love cannot face ... and that love can never come to an end.

# 18.
# GROUNDWORK

"You've got her!" That was not a quotation from the Marriage Service, although it referred to an equally demanding and fascinating undertaking. The actual words were spoken in a strange mixture of Polish and English to a dog-collared Welshman, sitting in an aircraft at the threshold of a runway. The aeroplane was improbably called a Chipmunk.

We were away at a summer camp with the Air Training Corps. It was the tail end of a day's flying. The previous night I had indulged in a verbal wrangle with a Polish flying instructor, when we put the world to rights and he wondered whether he would ever return to his country. Now at the end of that glorious day, during which for hour after hour he had taken our cadets aloft for flying experience, he was tired, thirsty and hungry, but for the sake of Polish and Welsh entente cordiale he invited me to join him for a final circuit and bump. Gladly I went.

I strapped myself firmly into the aircraft and then gazed at the array of instruments, most of which were still familiar to me. We arrived at the end of the runway, when the ominous words were spoken.

"You've got her!"

"I've got her!"

There had been no time for discussion

Instinctively, I checked all around to make certain that the field was clear, grabbed the stick in my right hand and, with the left, eased the throttle fully forward. As we began to veer off the runway, I applied the opposite pressure on the rudder bar, gently moved the stick back and was airborne. Five hundred feet up, a climbing turn to the left, I looked about at the countryside as it was unravelling itself beneath me.

It was a surprise that, after an interval of fifteen years, some of the simple art of flying was still alive. With time for only one circuit, around we went. The landing resembled a controlled crash and we rumbled our way back to the hangers.

"Finished for the day!"

Apparently, one such landing was enough for him. I invited my Polish friend for a free pint that evening. It had all been too brief an encounter with the past, but today is fondly remembered.

Back in the Parish, my feet were firmly on the ground. The parson is like a chameleon. In the same morning, you can share in the sadness of a funeral on the heels of the happiness of a wedding. There is no room for pretence or play acting; insincerity can be spotted a mile off. You learn to give every person your complete and absorbed attention. Somewhere I have read St. Augustine's comment that, "God loves us as though there were but one of us to love." That is a tough act for a human being to follow, but follow we must.

The death of Archbishop John Morgan was the end of a living legend for me. He was dying of cancer at St. Luke's Hospital in London. We were all aware of the great courage he had shown to travel to Llandaff Cathedral for a final celebration of the Eucharist. The occasion was the consecration of the new Bishop of Bangor.

At the high altar, Frank Jenkins, one of the Minor Canons, stood on one side of the Archbishop, whilst I was on the other. We were not there for any ceremonial reason. As the Service progressed, we took the Archbishop's weight and guided him through the Liturgy. He knew that it was the end and was magnificent. Back in London, he died a few days later. I remember him with love. It had been under his guidance that I had acquired my dog collar.

Evensong in the Cathedral drew a larger congregation on Saturday than on any other weekday. One particular evening, the Dean was late and Evensong was well under way, as he slipped quietly, but not unnoticed, into his stall. He was never late!

The music soared about the vaulted ceilings with the measured unfolding of the Psalms. The lessons echoed coherently around the pillars as the words disappeared into the distant corners. The anthem seemed to tip-toe with its precise beat. This was Anglican worship at its best.

To many people, the State Prayers may well sound like vain repetition, but for us they are integral to the fabric of the Service. That evening there was to be a dramatic change.

For many years we had prayed for Charles, Duke of Cornwall. That evening the Dean indicated that he would conduct the State Prayers and loud and clear came "Charles, Prince of Wales"! The Dean had just returned from Cardiff Arms Park and the closing ceremony of the Commonwealth Games, where the Queen had announced the great tidings for Wales. We must have been the first congregation to pray for Charles with his new title ... the Prince of Wales.

Much more care and thought is afforded these days to the parents of still-born children. In the previous century out of every ten births in a family at least six would die prematurely or immediately after the birth. It was good fortune if the remaining four were to reach puberty. Life was cheap. Half way through the twentieth century, the death rate was much diminished, but the care for the mother of the still-born had advanced little. Too often, she was left in the ward with the other mothers, as they nursed their new-born and all the chat was about new life.

One afternoon I found myself alongside my friend, Alun, with whom I shared much of my Air Training Corps activities. He was carrying a small box, which held the body of his still-born son. Alun and Prue had three lovely daughters and their hopes had been high. So we stood together at the family grave, as I committed this scrap of humanity into the love of God. I could understand the anger and bitterness which can devour the soul. Many times I was to hear the human cry, "Where is God in all this?" It is a fair question. My answer is simple, but hard to accept. "God is always right here with us and shares our tears." Even harder to accept was to be the death of Prue in a few years, leaving Alun alone with his three daughters.

At the end of most tragedies, the families thanked me for all that had been said and done. In my heart, I felt that I had actually said and done very little. Perhaps, after all the ache and the pain, God had been seen to be there, if only through the presence of the parson, a very pale shadow of God! I suspect that this is the way in which God does work, even though I was left with the thought that He could have achieved a higher profile. The parson needs encouragement too!

Our training for work in Mental Hospitals had been nil. This became painfully obvious when I was asked by a family to visit the large Institution at Whitchurch in Cardiff. The Victorians had built well with red brick in extensive grounds. The whole place was naturally enclosed by high walls and was hidden from the public gaze.

I was nervous as I plodded the long drive into the Hospital grounds. I had never been to a Mental Hospital. With me went all the overtones and misconceptions of the ignorant.

To my surprise, I walked unchallenged through the massive portals into the cathedral-like entrance hall. There were no locks in evidence. The lady at the reception desk headed me off in the right direction. I felt very young.

That place could have matched any maze and I was pleased when I finally reached the ward I needed. It was locked. I rang the bell and was admitted by a nurse who set me off again along a corridor. She abandoned me. All that I was looking for was a room number.

I was not alone. That corridor was full of ladies of all shapes and over-large sizes. Obviously I was the odd-ball and a novelty. All eyes were upon me. Then a formidable lady, built like a Cardiff front row forward with a hat on, emerged from the ruck. I stopped. She carried a massive handbag, which she waved with menace in my direction. I was beaten before a word was spoken. She seemed to grow larger.

"Pray for me."

"I will." It was a sort of whisper. I tried to escape.

"Pray now!"

I bowed my head and clasped my hands in preparation to make a serious supplication to God. She was not happy.

"On your knees!"

Down I went in total obedience ... no clergy training manual had mentioned the danger of assault. Her handbag was clutched to her bosom, whilst all the other ladies moved closer and they seemed to tower over me.

"Let us pray!"

I meant it! I have long forgotten the prayers that I used, but I am certain that my plight must have been noticed by God.

Twenty years later, I was to be responsible for a twelve-month interregnum at Rainhill, one of the largest mental institutions in the country. At least in that corridor, I had taken my first faltering step, even though I had ended on my knees ... not too bad a position for a parson! The next uncertain step was taken a few months later.

The sun was shining brightly one Sunday afternoon, as I responded to a request that I take a Service at Hensol Castle in the Vale of Glamorgan. A hundred or so seriously disturbed patients were housed there. D'rene and the children came along for the ride. Yet again there were large wrought iron gates to guard a long drive which led to the Castle, well away from the public gaze.

The Chapel stood apart like a parish church. I left D'rene to find seats. The place was full. We had not explained to the children what went on in Hensol Castle. I had never been there. I disappeared into the vestry.

At the stroke of three I processed, as lonely as a parson, to my pew. At least I looked the part ... in surplice, scarf and hood. I made a timorous start.

"Good afternoon everyone."

Their response was instant, like a clap of thunder.

"Good afternoon!"

This was brilliant. However, when I announced the opening hymn, one of the congregation jumped to her feet and made an announcement.

"It's holly, holly, holly again!"

There was a loud groan from the congregation, but it was too late. The organist had received my nod and was well into the opening bars of "Holy, holy, holy, Lord God Almighty". That episode ruined that hymn for me for ever.

The congregation was split into two parts. This was a piece of ecclesiastical choreography that I was not to meet again. The majority faced the altar and me. That was fine. However, D'rene and the children had found places behind the back row and, to my surprise, the patients on the two back rows had turned their chairs around to face my little family. My three youngsters were fascinated and even today it comes up in conversation. It had never occurred to us not to take them with us.

My daughter, Jane, was deeply puzzled by one lady who was nursing a doll throughout the whole proceedings. Incidentally, Jane was to work eventually in a mental hospital as an electro-encephalograph technician involved with brain scanning, a task well beyond my understanding. However, I know that such work demands sensitivity and the natural ability to calm a patient. Perhaps those qualities were initiated in Jane at Hensol Castle on that particular afternoon.

Summers in Llandaff were dominated by the Annual Music Festival, which lasted a full week after months of preparation, but as my role was to look after the parish life, my involvement in the Festival was marginal.

The music was tremendous and most evenings I sat behind a pillar in the Lady Chapel, absorbing quartets, quintets, orchestras and the whole Uncle Tom Cobley of music. The final Saturday evening was always the same ... the Treorchy Male Voice Choir. Not only were those the golden days of Welsh Rugby, we were also equally proud of our singing. It was a good time to be Welsh. "Myfanwy" was never sung like that and was never off the menu. It was a hymn with a special memory for me.

Years before, during my time in Southern Rhodesia, I was given five days leave from flying training. During my two years out there, it was to be my only break. The Rhodesians were very kind. I had put my name on the hospitality list and hoped for the best. It was to be quite a journey.

The two main cities were Bulawayo and Salisbury, which were separated by three hundred miles of nothing much. When we had arrived at Bulawayo, all potential aircrews were housed in the local cattle market. Our beds were neatly lined up in the cattle pens with a locker apiece and a canvas blind which we let down at night for privacy. The journey by train up from Durban through the Kalahari Desert via Johannesburg had been exhilarating, after being incarcerated for seven weeks in a troop ship, fed with endless Irish stew, even in the Red Sea. No wonder that cattle pen was privacy and a home!. The first Sunday in Bulawayo, I joined St. John's Church Choir and, being Welsh, was sharply enrolled into the local Male Voice Choir and, to my amazement, found myself three days later on stage for a performance of the Elijah. I kept a low and rather silent profile in the back row.

That hospitality list came up trumps. Before moving on to an advanced flying course, I was off on my five-day leave. I travelled in the guard's van of a goods train heading south from Salisbury. Seventy miles on, I was deposited at the trackside. The train disappeared. The horizon was endless scrub with not a soul in sight. I felt lonely.

The land was not entirely flat, as little hills dotted the vista, like pimples. Such a ridiculously small hillock had killed my room-mate, Bob Dowen, a few weeks before. At night, foolishly out of fuel and too low to take to his parachute, both he and an experienced instructor had attempted a crash landing in the dark. It had been a barren and lonely place to die.

At last a small dust cloud moved towards me and I clambered into the back of a truck, as we set out for some twenty miles on an earthen-corrugated road. At forty the vehicle skimmed the tops of the corrugations. Below that speed, it was like being vibrated in a spin drier, not that I would have heard of such a machine in those days. My five days were to be spent on a tobacco farm.

The welcome was fantastic. Mine hosts chanced to be Welsh! After the first World War, this farmer had taken his gratuity and come to Rhodesia. There he learned his trade the hard way, carving a farm out of the inhospitable land. His home was still little more than wooden poles with white-washed canvas walls and a straw roof. All our R.A.F. accommodation was built in the same way, but on the farm there was the odd rug or two on the concrete floors. Life was uncomplicated.

Truth must be stranger than fiction. We chatted about Wales as only exiles can. Our memories grew in the telling. The hillsides were greener and the hilltops more welcoming. That was when I discovered that my mother had taught him in school in Pontypridd. This was a six thousand mile coincidence, which enabled us to chat about "teacher Winnie".

I suspected that they had lived too long in isolation. Five months before, their grand-daughter had been born. With pride, they showed me a photograph of the family in Gwelo. The inscription on the back looked all wrong. They had spelt Myfanwy incorrectly.

Sitting behind that pillar in Llandaff Cathedral, my memories returned to Rhodesia, as the ancient stones echoed to the lilt of Myfanwy, and the top tenors from Treorchy tore our hearts with melody.

The Festivals of Music came and went, but one smile remained long after the sounds had departed. The Dean had set out to meet the world-famous conductor, Claudio Arrau. The train at Cardiff General was late and time was pressing. At last, the great man arrived and announced that he was starving. The Dean stopped off at the Angel Hotel. Arrau must not have eaten for a week and placed a world-sized order. The Dean quietly peeped into his wallet and promptly ordered a soup and a roll for himself. This was the pre-credit card era.

The Lenten plays from my Tremorfa days were resurrected. The stage was set under the arch of the Pulpitum, which held the tremendous figure of Christ in Majesty. Nothing could have been more perfect. I knew that the youngsters who took part would never forget such an experience. Of course, the old formula of using as many children as possible proved to be a winner. I hoped that we all found new light in the Gospel stories, as they were acted in such a wonderful setting.

As with many a Parish Magazine, the Llandaff one was a perfect example of "as it was in the beginning, is now, and ever shall be". I needed help. It came from Charlie Chubb.

Most mornings, Charlie was up before dawn at work on the telephone in his back bedroom. Charlie was into nuts ... cobs and brazils and walnuts and others that I had never heard about. Fax machines and computers would have been a blessing for Charlie, as he battled on his telephone in the back bedroom into the small hours, calling contacts about the world. He never saw a nut! He was a sort of middle-middle nut-man, working at half of one per cent. Charlie located the nuts, bought them and sold them, and reaped his modest rewards.

"I live off peanuts!"

Above all, Charlie Chubb was a known character in the business world and that was his value to me. I needed help to improve the magazine.

Together we toured the Cardiff printers and in the back streets of Grangetown, we found Arthur Sansom of Qualitex. We all spoke the same language and a deal was made, which has lasted to the present day, naturally with inflation built into the system. Arthur has always lived up to the name of his firm. I was a little sad that I was not expected to write for the magazine, although it was probably all the better for that.

The Cathedral was well used by 'steam radio' as we were able to produce the sound quality acceptable for the mass media ... and, we hoped, for God! We were all expected to play our part and we quickly learned to ignore the glare of the lights, when television arrived, and to avoid trolleyed cameras and miles of cables. At least the "steam radio" hardly created any difficulty, as the Cathedral was wired for sound and the technicians were out of sight.

One Easter, I read the second lesson at Evensong. The passage was taken from the Gospel according to St. John and included verse 38, which describes how Joseph of Arimathea went to Pilate to claim the body of Jesus for burial, but did so in secret "for fear of the Jews". Maybe we should not have been surprised when two days later the letters arrived accusing us of anti-Semitism! Others found faults with the choir and one actually criticised a pause for breath in the middle of the prayers. Such responses were normal.

The temptation to reply with rudeness was very strong. We pictured these characters poised with pen and paper, week by week, hell-bent on criticism. Sadly they missed the whole point of the broadcasts and must have become spiritually immune to them.

The visitors continued to pour into the village of Llandaff and in droves found their way down the hill to the Cathedral. The building sits on the edge of the River Taff, the original bed of which must have been tight up against the walls of the Cathedral because in the present graveyard, just a few feet down, can be found the rounded, washed pebbles where the water had flowed in the past centuries. It was easy to imagine that ships were tied up alongside in ages past, where worship had continued for almost fourteen-hundred years and parsons like me had spent their days visiting folk in their cottages in the village up the hill. Some external things may change, but the heartbeat of worship and prayer is unceasing.

However, we are not immortal. Mother-in-law was rushed into hospital for major surgery. The timing was awkward. I was scheduled to conduct a Retreat for the Diocesan Anglican Young People's Association in Shrewsbury.

The Association agreed that I might bring Stephen and Jane with me, leaving D'rene and Martin to stand by at the hospital. It worked well. Off we went to a private school at Bomere Heath outside Shrewsbury. That four days could have been difficult, but three girls from my old parish in Cwmdare readily adopted my two little orphans.

They had a great time. I saw them at meals, scrubbed and fully dressed. I was redundant. The sun shone. The daily frolic involved the hose pipe in the garden. When I look back today at the notes of my addresses at that Retreat, that hose ought to have been turned on me. I can only conclude that the fun of being away together was what had ensured a success for that four days in the sun.

Happily mother-in-law survived her ordeal and went on to live an active life for a further fifteen years. Apparently I could do little wrong in her eyes and she often accompanied me in the car on my rounds. At many a meeting, she sat on the back row and was the butt of my stories. She was full of fun and was well received wherever we went together. She was a remarkable lady and we were good friends. Mothers-in-law are a much maligned race, which is a bit hard because every mother is odds on to become one. It is very fortunate that fathers-in-law are ignored.

We found ourselves on a steady treadmill with the round of worship controlling my days, only relieved by a weekly visit on Friday afternoons to visit our parents in Llanharan. In those days, we curates had to serve at least ten years before there was any hope of being appointed for a "living", as having a parish of one's own is euphemistically called.

Llandaff was a great place to work. The people could not have been kinder. The Dean was a hard task-master and led by example. His sermons should have been committed to print. It was perfect training for what was ahead of me.

The Church in Wales in those days seemed to be totally introverted and parochially minded. There was little encouragement even to move to another Diocese within the Province and to cross the border to England was regarded as mortal sin. Such a narrow system encouraged the curates to keep in line, touch their forelocks and wait for the Mighty Reaper to move the system along a bit, so that we might climb up the ladder of obedience and eventually find preferment. Most of us thought it intolerable and I was no exception.

Aged thirty-five, with three children, and with no prospect of becoming an incumbent for at least two years, even though we were happy at Llandaff, the inevitable cancer of frustration began to eat away.

# 19.
# CROSSROADS

Holidays were not the great travel experiences such as are commonplace today. The Costa Lottas had not mushroomed. Islands were still islands and not resorts and as most men drank mild or bitter, the lager lout had not been invented. The government even told one how much money could be taken abroad. Plastics, man-made fibres and biro pens were deemed to be excitement enough for us. Cigarette smoking was 'fashionable', 'grass' was mown, 'coke' was kept in the coal house, a 'joint' was a piece of meat and 'pot' was something you cooked in. The 'permissive society' was still underground.

We enjoyed two summer breaks in Tenby, two beaches and a lifeboat, ninety miles away in the outer reaches of West Wales. We shared accommodation one year with our extended family and the next year with the Armitages from Llandaff. It was a bucket and spade extravaganza.

Stephen brought ashore his first fish. We had set out for the beach at dawn and, flushed with success, rushed back to our quarters above a shop in Tenby High Street ... with our catch! We awoke the household to admire the exhibit ... a plaice about three inches long.

With ceremony, D'rene cleaned and cooked and presented the trophy to Stephen, who at the age of five would have preferred it stuffed and encased for posterity. The whole episode was treated as an undercover operation as the flat that we had rented was above a wet-fish shop. We kept our triumph to ourselves to avoid eviction.

There was another summer when we thought that we had struck oil, won the pools and broken the bank. We were invited to take a flat in Bournemouth, which was better than oil, the pools or the bank. A letter had arrived from a lady whom I had no recollection of meeting. Apparently she had been a visitor to the Cathedral and had much enjoyed my chat show on the superiority of the Welsh over the English. Our patter for the tourists and the pilgrims was well spiced with anecdotes and fulsome praise for the Welsh. Obviously, I had much impressed my benefactor.

The only charge required for the fourteen day occupancy of her holiday flat was a request that I preached a Sunday sermon in her Parish Church. As every parson has at least one sermon, proven and well worn, we accepted the offer with alacrity.

Everyone assured us that Bournemouth was a lovely place. That might well be correct. The first week it rained a lot of rain. D'rene was still involved in what she called her "seven year nappy wash" as we struggled to survive in the damp. The weather could only improve and the second week started with promise of doing just that. We had been given the usage of a beach hut on the edge of the shore. However, all was not well. The winds blew strong and hard off the sea for that entire week, keeping the grey waters tight against the promenade walls. We never saw any sand. All week we sat on the concrete, ate off a primus stove and returned to the flat for the next nappy wash. No wonder our children are convinced to this day that Bournemouth is basically inland and entirely damp.

Each morning of those fourteen days I waited for the postman. This was to be the letter that would turn our lives upside down. My old friend, Gwynno, the Archdeacon of Llandaff, had indicated that I was in line for the living of Bargoed.

I had never been to Bargoed, way up in the Rhymney Valley. There would not have been the possibility of such a visit, until it was dangled as the promised land. So prior to the Bournemouth holiday, we had set out to reconnoitre. I was disguised cunningly behind a tie. Our world was aglow with expectation as we traversed the hills and the dales, heading for Bargoed.

The Vicarage was exceptionally large and exciting, set apart from the rest of mankind in a sort of field, which in the last century would have been the garden. We peeped through the windows, worked out the rooms and began to plan our furniture. This was fun. The Parish of Bargoed stretched out down the valley with streets covered in gold and coal dust. It was beautiful.

My spy in the ecclesiastical system was Bob White, the Head Verger in the Cathedral.

"Don't worry, Bob", he said to me. "I'll have the news before they know it themselves."

"Catch the first post you can."

"Don't worry."

Bob was the perfect mole in touch with every nuance of episcopal whim. He would surely write to me with the inside information.

"The cards are stacked in your favour."

That letter never came. A man from West Wales was appointed, who was already a Vicar. There was to be no explanation. My mole had failed. We never visited Bargoed again.

Life went on in both the Cathedral and the Parish. Services were dovetailed and trimmed like packs of sausages. We clergy waited in the side aisles and, on cue, processed to the high altar to cope with the next hundred-plus communicants. Stewards and vergers moved chairs and lecterns and assorted gaggles of congregations into standard sized packages of worshippers. The Cathedral shop and the Prebendal House tea room competed for their coach-carried customers.

One afternoon we all had tea with Bert and Lena, who were real friends of ours in Llandaff. They had both shown us much kindness. That afternoon, we met Lena's brother-in-law, Noel Thomas, who was the Chaplain Superintendent of the Mersey Mission to Seamen in Liverpool. I had not heard of the organisation.

On reflection, when I had been curate in the Parish of Roath, the Cardiff Missions to Seamen Chaplain, Gerald Morgan, had invited me to join him on a trip to sea.

We had driven to Barry and were taken by launch to visit the lighthouse keepers on Flatholm in the middle of the Bristol Channel. It had been a fabulous day when the sun had shone and the sea was kind. So often I had gazed across the waters to the islands of Flatholm and Steepholm, trying to imagine life away from the mainland, and I realised that the journey that day was to be a great privilege.

Getting ashore at Flatholm was not easy and we wondered whether the return would be possible. Jumping from a moving craft on to the small quay was obviously easier than the reverse operation. The island seemed much bigger as we walked up to the light-house.

Everything was spotless, polished and, naturally, Bristol fashion. The light-house men were delighted to have visitors. We laughed and joked and climbed to the top of the light and it was obvious that they wished to share the pride they spent on their work. Finally, before we departed, we bowed our heads and joined in prayer. It was simple, sincere and natural. For the first time I sang the old seafarers' hymn, Eternal Father, with a glint of understanding. This was a moving experience.

Then I forgot all about it as the years went by ... the Missions to Seamen had nothing to do with me.

It was about seven years after the Flatholm excursion that I received a letter from the Reverend Noel Thomas asking that I consider being an assistant chaplain in the Mersey Mission to Seamen in Liverpool. Such a thought had never occurred to me, but the invitation was warm and friendly; so we decided that there would be no harm in making a visit to the North-West. It was the courteous thing to do.

Whilst I was aware that Cardiff was a port and in its heyday had been a major coal-exporting centre, I knew that all that was lost in history. The port in Cardiff had little impact on our lives. We never saw any ships and I knew nothing about seafaring.

D'rene's first job on leaving College had been in a shipping office in Mountstewart Square in the heart of the notorious Tiger Bay, when Shirley Bassey was a Sunday School teacher and sin was flaunted on the streets. With nods and winks, we all thought that we knew about the "goings-on" in Tiger Bay. This questionable way of life was fifteen miles from our respectable little home village of Llanharan. The journey to work in Cardiff had involved D'rene in a two-train journey. When Cardiff General station was bombed during the war, D'rene actually walked six miles to work from Ely station, so D'rene, at least, had some knowledge of the docks and its multi-coloured population. I knew nothing about ships or seafarers and assumed that they would play no part in my life.

Liverpool was a great surprise to us. We were whisked around the thirty-six miles of water-front to wonder at the sizes and nationalities of about two hundred ships. It was exciting and the little boy in me began to bubble. We enjoyed seeing the Mersey Mission's brand new headquarters, called Kingston House, in the shadow of Pier Head and the famous Liver Building. We stayed in Merchant Navy House, which was the Mission's Club for Officers. There we were spoiled and well looked after. Of course, I was fascinated and forgot that first sight is rarely twenty-twenty.

Back in Llandaff, we thought and talked. We did not know how to sort out our minds for such a traumatic move. I was ignorant of the nature of the work. Liverpool was two hundred miles from our families' homes and friends. Surrounded by such indecision, we concluded that it had been a mere whisper of a call. We stayed in Llandaff and quietly forgot about the North-West and all things nautical.

Life continued as though nothing had happened. I watched the movement of clergy in the Diocese and worked out the league table for the probable preferments. My calculations proved that there might be another three years before I was given a parish to call my own. In those days in Wales, it was normal for a curate to wait for about twelve years before being appointed as vicar. Today the average time is reduced to about four.

Ten men had been ordained with me in 1950 on the same day and I realised that already nine of them had left the Church in Wales to work in England. The inference was obvious. Sitting tight and hoping for the best was the recipe for despair. Financially a move to England would be of little advantage, but mentally I knew that "over the border" a greater sense of freedom was enjoyed by the clergy, not to be encountered in Wales. That Liverpool trip had unsettled me! It is hard to live with frustration. In my heart I was realising that life could not meander on ... action was required.

When we had returned that first time from Liverpool, we had crossed the Brecon Beacons and dropped into Aberdare to have a cup of tea with our good friend Esther. The front door, as ever, was unlocked and open and we were received like Royalty. On the way back home from Liverpool we had decided that we would tell no-one about our travels up North and that was to include Esther.

There was a blazing coal fire in the back kitchen with its shining black-leaded grate. The kettle was immediately moved across on its hob and the tea was almost instant. We all sat back for a nostalgic chat about my days as curate in Cwmdare and to catch up on the deaths, births and marriages. There is nothing like a spot of gossipy nostalgia. We Welsh are good at it.

A bang on the front door and a shout sent Esther scurrying out in her wrap-around apron and slippered feet to greet the caller. She had recognised the voice and had headed off its owner into the front parlour. Minutes later she was back, cleared the tea things off the table and suggested to D'rene that the men were better left on their own. Men have simple minds and have no idea that they are being manipulated.

I lit my pipe and Will pulled out a fag, as we launched out into a happily shared eulogy on the wonders of the Welsh Rugby side. We were wallowing in the golden years at Cardiff Arms Park and words came easily.

Unknown to us mere mortals of men, Daisy Green had arrived and had taken up residence in the sanctuary of the front parlour. She operated behind closed doors!

Daisy was a legend in her own lifetime. During my years as the curate of Cwmdare, I was not expected to be aware of her peculiar gifts, or of her activities on my patch. I had dubbed her, with affection, the local 'witch'. Every village has one. Daisy was observed to have the special sight, concentrating her beams on cups. It was, of course, without doubt, I thought, probably, nonsense. That was my official line and I was expected to stick to it.

Daisy was short, plump and jolly. There could be no question of her arriving by broom-stick. However, she did have cats. They were black and firmly into breeding and not in the least sinister, except maybe to other cats. We loved Daisy, as she waddled the streets and, if she was casting spells, it was all done with beatific smiles. I have no idea what a twentieth century witch should wear, but Daisy looked comfortably Welsh. She had a round look about her and was endowed with the ability to settle into every corner of a chair, like the incoming tide. Her slippered feet moved to port and starboard just in time to prevent her over-turning. Daisy could honestly be called a character.

During my Cwmdare days, I had grown very close to her. Her aged mother had died in my first months in the Parish. That old lady had barely tolerated my ministrations, as she faced death curled up in the front parlour with the bed on blocks of wood, which enabled her to look down the valley and dream of her youth wondrously again. She had died with a distant smile and the aura of a Romany. The Valley knew that she was not like the rest of us. I felt the same about her. She had passed her wisdom on to Daisy.

Daisy's husband, Will, had died of cancer. In my mind, I see him now. He lay there firmly tucked into a large bed, which filled the parlour and left room for the aspidistra and one visitor at a time and "not too long, please". Stiff as a board, there was Will, white and weak, ready for the undertaker, waving his handkerchief at all his visitors. We were not sure whether he was saying farewell or indicating surrender. He did not speak. Will was the gentlest of Christian souls and, with a final wave, he was gone.

Daisy Green and I had shared pain and sadness and had become friends, but, when I was with her, the teacups were for drinking tea! I ignored her cats, even though they sat in a line and smiled at me.

That evening of our return from Liverpool, Esther had rescued my cup off the tea tray and had smuggled it into the parlour, out of the sight and sound of the men. There the tea dregs were apparently whirled around and the cup upturned into the saucer. D'rene and Esther had awaited her pronouncements. On the way back home to Llandaff, D'rene reported it all to me and we laughed.

Daisy had seen my future in the tea leaves. It was all to do with water. I was to wear a peak cap and would travel under water. She did not attempt to explain that. Then she described the house we would occupy ... three steps up under an arch to the front door. D'rene and I knew that it was all complete nonsense.

Here was a lady who had never travelled more than a handful of miles from Aberdare. I cannot explain her remarks. All that I can do is record the facts.

Within six months, I received another pressing invitation to move to Liverpool and this time I knew that it was serious. There had been no movement of clergy in the diocese and my future in the Church in Wales seemed blank of hope.

Three months after that, we were in Liverpool, January 1961. The Mission to Seamen chaplains at that time wore Naval type caps. I was certainly working either side of water, Liverpool and Birkenhead, and almost daily passed under the Mersey through the tunnel. We did find a house in Aigburth with three steps up to the front door and, of course, there was an arch! Perhaps, maybe, Daisy had seen the future. Each one of her pronouncements had been correct!

After that second call to Liverpool, I had given the Dean the obligatory three months notice, knowing I was in for a difficult time.

The folk in Llandaff were surprised and looked at me with astonishment when the word Liverpool was mentioned. Most seemed to regard it as in outer space. The Headmaster of the Cathedral School shook my hand and then his head, regretting, he said, that he lacked the courage to undertake such an enterprise himself. I began to feel like a latter day David Livingstone on my way to deepest darkness. Many expressed such thoughts. Some clergy told me bluntly that I was a fool as I was "well placed" in the Cathedral with my future in the Diocese assured. I admitted that I was puzzled by such comments, but happily was not deterred.

The Bishop was not pleased with our decision to move to England and went out of his way to express himself. Obviously our paths crossed each morning in the Cathedral, as we all shared the daily round of Services. For the three months of my notice, the Bishop ignored me. Even at the crack of dawn on my last Christmas morning when we chanced to arrive at the West door together and I opened it for him, wishing him the compliments of the Season, to my surprise he looked straight at me and with a grunt pushed past. It was sad to reflect that after ten years of single-minded service in the Diocese, it was all to end with a grunt. In truth, I should not have been too taken aback, as his response to my letter of resignation was that I was not ever to consider any return to his Diocese. The boats were burned.

That Christmas of 1960 was deeply sad, as D'rene's father had died a few days before the Festival and had actually been buried on Christmas Eve. A month later we were in Liverpool.

Mother-in-law came with us and with six aboard we chugged over the Brecon Beacons amidst the winter snow into a strange new world. Much of what we held dear was left behind and all that we had was the family, our goods and chattels. In the end that proved to be all that was needed.

Llandaff had given me much more than I could possibly have repaid. I know of no better way to see your life in perspective than to kneel at the crack of dawn in the depth of winter in a cold Cathedral with your knee caps hurting and an empty tummy. Perspective reminded you that man had worshipped God in that place for over fourteen hundred years. At least I discovered that God could not possibly have any interest in knee caps and breakfast. It taught me to be patient as folk trotted out their woes and worries, as though they alone had problems in life. The patience of God with the grumbles of men must be infinite ... it was a thought worthy of meditation.

The Dean of Llandaff, Eryl Thomas, had taught me my trade as a parson, not only when he had been the Warden of the Theological College, but by his example and expertise as a parish priest. The foundations for the Liverpool years were well in place.

A real sadness was that it marked the end of the on-going saga of Charlie the Mouse. I was long to remember the enthusiasm of those children for my mythical mouse. I had grown used to the youngsters charging into the Cathedral to grab the front seats, mowing down the emerging nine-o-clockers in the process. Charlie had dominated my life in Llandaff.

One Sunday morning, I had been standing at the West door, wishing everyone farewell until the following Sunday, when a father with two children asked if he might have a word. He introduced himself as Wojnarowski. Later in Liverpool I was to become quite accustomed to such convoluted names ending in "owski". He was Polish.

During the war, he had escaped from Poland and found his way to England. He joined the Royal Air Force and had been a pilot of a Lancaster bomber. We became good friends. His request was that I might sit as a model for a sculpture of St. Giles for a church of that name in Oxford. He explained that St. Giles was known for his love of children and therefore he saw me as a likely victim for the role. I agreed, but did point out that the saint was also associated with cripples, beggars and blacksmiths!

His studio was the garage at his home. There we chatted away as I wondered at his skill. He was a part-time lecturer at the Art College in Cardiff Castle. I discovered that, when he was demobbed, he had become involved in sending food parcels from America to Europe and had made much money. The whole experience had convinced him that money was not a sufficient motivation in life; so he became an art teacher. I was intrigued as he built the head, piece by piece, with clay. Unfortunately I was not to see the completed work, but he did offer me one of his sculptures as a reward for patience.

One of my proudest possessions is a beautifully carved head of a Negro, kept as a reminder of Wojnarowski and of the happy days when Charlie was the best known mouse in the Diocese of Llandaff.

# 20.
# HOME

Transference from Parish Priest to Missions to Seamen Chaplain was obviously not going to be instantly easy, but nothing had prepared me for the trauma of leaving the spiritual treadmill of Cathedral life. I felt that I had been abandoned in a desert. We still kept the discipline of Matins and Evensong, though there were never any seafarers present and it seemed like worship in a vacuum. There obviously was to be no natural community as in a parish, which would have made me feel welcomed and needed. It was as though I was cut off from humanity. The result was that, from the very first day, I was uncertain about the future and suspected that I was not the man for the job.

The Chaplain Superintendent was a kind and gentle character with a wealth of experience in the work. For many years, he had served in Santos in South America and in Southampton. Kind though Noel Thomas was, he utterly failed in showing me how to visit a ship and in that process to discover what made a seafarer. Noel appeared to live locked away in his study and, apart from the daily worship, we did not meet. Above all, his life seemed to be dominated by the mysterious Monthly Committee Meeting.

The Committee of the Mersey Mission to Seamen was the body of trustees with the final responsibility for the well-being of the Mission. It was a self-appointing body, a good blend of clerics and professional business men. At this stage I had not met them and it was not expected that the Assistant Chaplains should have any contact.

Unknown to me, Noel was not finding the work in Liverpool to his liking and was by that time at odds with the Committee. This showed in the way in which for days before each meeting he was on edge and in distress. All this tension was not understood by me, as I attempted to discover why I was in Liverpool and whether I had made the right decision. I was not a happy man.

The Mersey Mission to Seamen,
Kingston House, James Street, Liverpool

The headquarters of the Mission was called Kingston House. It was just four years old, well sited in James Street, adjacent to Pier Head and the famous water frontage of Liverpool.

The building had been designed by Canon Bill Evans, who had done tremendous work for over two decades and had been awarded the M.B.E. for his wartime contribution to the life of the port. During his time, the Mission had spread its care for seafarers throughout Merseyside with nine buildings, all established to meet the wartime needs of the seafarer ashore.

The post-war years in Liverpool were different, in that the opposite problem had to be faced of winding down from the wartime high and, in doing just that, there was an atmosphere of failure.

Bill Evans had built Kingston House on his well proven past experience, but he could not have foreseen the changes ahead. He had assumed that the pre-war class system would prevail and that social activity would be as before. All was not well in Kingston House.

The other assistant chaplain was Charlie Walker. Charlie was larger than life. He was a Scouser, full of humour, anecdotes and nervousness. Charlie was not happy in his work. For two years he had plodded on in the Mission and was defeated by all that was about him. His pent-up frustrations poured over me and, as much as anything, pulled me down into despondency.

Charlie and I only observed as the Committee appeared each month, disappeared into the fourth floor board-room and then departed for another four weeks. We knew nothing of the conflict.

There were strange rules, which we were asked to note and obey. We were not allowed into the Officers' Lounge Bar at any time. That place was the responsibility of the Chaplain Superintendent. Charlie and I were condemned to use our shared office, in a back room on the ground floor, amongst the beer barrels, alongside the tradesmen's entrance. We were allowed to use the Seamen's Canteen, which was graced with concrete tables designed for the rough usage of the seamen and the rough assistant chaplains! This was a long way from the ethereal atmosphere of Llandaff Cathedral. What was I doing in Liverpool!

The common seamen were not expected to use the billiard room with its two tables and we correctly assumed that the ban applied to us ... at least we might have been allowed to chat to the players.

Our work was controlled by the clock and not by the demands of the ministry. One day we worked from nine to six and then on the next day there was a split shift, nine to one and six to ten. That evening shift was very tiresome as we were not allowed anywhere in the building except, of course, our dungeon study and the empty Canteen with its concrete tables. Life was so dull!

After the hectic round of Cathedral life where we had started at seven in the morning and made use of the whole day, this attempt to impose hours seemed infantile and totally unproductive. I was becoming desperate.

The only bright spot was Charlie Walker, my fellow assistant chaplain, who proved to be an excellent ship visitor. From him I learned how to handle the nations of the world. He smiled with good cheer, a thick skin and perfect timing ... he knew when to linger with intent and when to pass on quickly. He taught me how to turn a blind eye on an embarrassing situation and how to be selectively deaf. We were proving to be a good team aboard the ships, but we knew that our hands were tied by the impossible restrictions imposed upon us in Kingston House.

The club had little to offer and compared with the other seafaring organisations in Liverpool it was a failure. Up the road in Hardman Street, the Roman Catholics ran the Stella Maris Club in Atlantic House. Each day, there was a bundle of activity, dances every evening and sleeping accommodation for over a hundred men. The place was well used and loved by seafarers around the world. The result of all this was that Charlie and I crept around the docks afraid to mention the non-activity in Kingston House. The subject was better avoided, as the seaman was well able to express his thoughts. In silence, we could only agree that the situation in Kingston House was worse than they could imagine.

We honestly did our best. Charlie fed me the information from his experience and with the enthusiasm of ignorance, I put the ideas forward. Noel blocked the lot. Nothing was to change and we were to keep in line. He assured us that we did not understand the needs of the seafarer. The only advice that he gave us was to "get out amongst the men". He never explained the how and the why of such activity.

So at last I began to realise that there was no way in which I could continue and that frustration was leading to despair. I was finally ready to admit defeat.

All this misery must have made me blind to the effect the situation was having upon D'rene and the family. I thought that I was containing my problems and leaving them at Pier Head at the end of each day. Obviously, D'rene had found life much different in Liverpool.

Our home was on one side of a busy dual carriage-way. This meant that we never saw the folk who lived opposite and were only vaguely aware of our next door neighbours. The people next door but one were never seen. No-one called at our house. We knew no-one. We had become accustomed to meeting people in a parish and being known in our community. In Liverpool, we lived like everyone else. It was strange.

We did our best to find beaches for the children. The local Merseyside coast was untenable with oil and sewage. There was one day when we ventured as far as Rhyl. We did find a concrete promenade with its mish-mash of kiosks and fried onion stands. We stayed for an hour amidst the hundreds of lost souls, wandering the canned music arcades. After the secluded sandy beaches of South Wales, we wrote off the North in one day!

*D'rene, Martin, Stephen, and Jane ... on a South Wales beach!*

Stephen and Jane settled into the local primary school quite happily. Young Martin helped his mother by painting the skirting boards. I plodded off to work each day and kept my head in the sand. It could not last.

The crunch came when I arrived home one evening at ten thirty to find the house in complete darkness; D'rene and the children were in bed. A letter faced me on the breakfast room table. It stopped me in my tracks.

D'rene had also reached the end. It was spelt out in the simplest of language with no room for compromise. It was the required catalyst. Obviously I had stopped communicating and she could take no more of our life in Liverpool. All that I felt was relief. At last, I could talk.

Words tumbled out as we revealed our inner thoughts. Stupidly, J had assumed that I had concealed my misery, but all that I had achieved was to reduce D'rene to despair. It was time for positive action. We both accepted that we were finished with Liverpool and with the Mersey Mission to Seamen. We smiled again, knowing that whatever lay ahead we would face it together. It seemed natural to return to Wales.

Next day I wrote to Gwynno James, the Archdeacon of Llandaff, telling my sorry tale and asked that I might be considered for a living in the Diocese of Llandaff. The reply was instant and was not much more than one sentence.

"Try Ynysybwl!"

That was not the brush off, but a genuine suggestion.

I knew roughly where that improbable name was on the map. At least it was on the map, if the scale was large enough! It was a mining village, near to Pontypridd. My topographical book on South Wales had little to say.

"Pop. 4,849. An industrial town 3 miles north of Pontypridd, situated at the head of a small valley called Cwm Clydach. Christ Church was erected in 1886. To the west of the town is Cae Maen, near Mynachdy, which name seems to imply the existence of an ancient cell."

We knew all about such places as Ynysybwl ... so we thought.

This was to be the solution of all our problems and an escape from the North-West. D'rene and I never stopped talking about our good fortune and our dreams for the future. Any place seemed rose-coloured, as we prepared to shake off the dust of Liverpool.

At last, the chance came for a few days off and, telling no-one in Liverpool of our intentions, we set out for South Wales. The journey in those days took eight hours. As ever, we all squeezed into mother-in-law's home at Llanharan. This was our opportunity to visit for the very first time the promised land of Ynysybwl. We were happy.

It was a sunny day for the adventure. There was no difficulty in spotting the sign-post bearing the name with no vowels. Suddenly we were there.

This village valley was like any other. The little church was well placed in the centre and it looked inviting, water-tight, cared for and loved and, of course, shut.

"Excuse me, but could you direct us to the vicarage, please?"

A puzzled look crossed the stranger's brow and she accosted another passer-by.

"Where's the vicarage, love?"

"He's gone."

They both turned to me, as though I was responsible for the cleric's departure. I followed the lead that had been given and persevered.

"Where did he live before he left?"

"Try the post office, bach."

All this mystery should have prepared us.

We were directed up the hill out of the village. They suggested that we could not miss it.

"Just keep going. It's a good bit out, opposite a pub."

"What's the name of the pub?"

"It's closed!"

An empty vicarage and a closed pub seemed a sad combination, as we pressed forward and very much up-ward.

The village was left far behind before we spotted our destination. We had begun to giggle and throw out witty comments. It was really nervous hysteria.

"It's a long way to get the milk."

"We'll buy a cow."

"It'll not get up the hill!"

It was a good Welsh two miles in third gear. We knew that we had arrived because on one side of the road was a broken down pub and a sad wind-blown house on the other. We all knew why the previous incumbent had slung his hook. There was not a soul in sight, apart from the sheep.

The front door opened on to the mountain road and nothing indicated that it was a vicarage. The back garden was open tundra, well grazed by sheep and polished by the wind. This was another world, where time had stopped and mankind had fled for a better place.

The children were intrigued by the small outhouse with a swinging door, at the bottom of the plot.

"It's the Ty Bach".

Welsh comedians made their living with colourful and noisy tales about the Ty Bach, "the little house", the classical Welsh outside toilet. Here was a splendid example.

It was a two seater. As we gazed, we told the children of the good old days in the depth of winter, setting out at night through the snow.

"Tie some string to the back door, so you can find your way back when the candle blows out."

They thought we were in cloud cuckoo land.

We walked about the vicarage and peered through the panes with total disbelief and knew that there was no need for a family vote on our future. Yet, it was a place of wonder. The hills folded about us, tinged with conifers. The mountain above was aglow with heather and, down below, sprawled Ynysybwl in all its glory, but I knew that never was I to be the next Vicar of that place. As a family, we smiled at that thought.

Back in Liverpool, we soldiered on with a great sense of togetherness. The decision had been taken to find a way out of the job which was no longer acceptable to me or the family.

I put my cards on the table. The Honorary Secretary of the Mersey Mission was Dick Hodges, a director of Elder Dempster Shipping Company. We had barely exchanged a word with each other in my six months sojourn there, but I felt that he was the person whom I could approach for advice and explain my reasons for wishing to leave Merseyside. To have spoken to the Chairman would really have been too formal. It seemed wrong to do no more than seek advice.

Dick Hodges was a tall, well-built character conveying the impression that he could quell a rebellion with a twitch of his eyebrows. Happily there was no twitch as I expressed my thoughts about my future and the lack of it in the Mission. Later, I was to discover that his responsibility was the selection and control of staff for his Company on a worldwide scale. He had no qualms in handling my problems. I told my tale of woe. He seemed not in the least surprised at the picture that I was painting. His advice was to take no action until the New Year, which was only a few months away. This I accepted as we had no desire to uproot ourselves over Christmas.

Unknown to me, the Committee was busy making moves about the future of the Mission, as not one member had confidence in the regime under which I was so unhappy. I had told Dick Hodges nothing new.

The Committee had waited for three years for the situation to improve and the time had come for a firm decision to be made. A few days after my discussion, the October Committee meeting, after consultation with the Bishop of Liverpool, had passed a vote of no confidence. Noel Thomas had resigned immediately. Actually he must have been much relieved and, happily, within a few weeks, he was appointed Vicar of Harwich. That was a good decision and he fulfilled an excellent ministry there. His three years at the Mission had not been kind to him and the rest of us had been caught in the cross-fire. Suddenly, I understood the problems of Noel Thomas and how they had washed over us. Everything had been wrong.

A telephone call and I found myself at Binns Road in the board-room of Crawfords Biscuits being interviewed by the Chairman of the Mission, Donald Crawford. To my utter astonishment, the appointment as Chaplain Superintendent was mine, if I wished.

Here was a dilemma. At no time had I thought that my future lay in the docks of Liverpool and nothing in my background had suggested that this was to be my vocation. My intention had been to stay in the Mission for a couple of years and then return to parish life. All that I had ever wished to be was a parish priest.

Donald Crawford was persuasive. He pointed out that I had discovered the basic problems in the Mission and that, during my short time, I must have pondered on the proper role of the chaplain in the port.

"Your frustrations must have revealed what you wish to do. You already know the answers!"

To my surprise, I felt that this was true and that in the past painful months I had developed a clear idea of solutions for the difficulties and had plans for the future. That had been my main preoccupation during all those months. Perhaps I was well placed to take over the Mission! I had been long convinced that what was required were the skills of a parish priest and a firm control over the business side of the Mission.

I had obviously played no part in the departure of Noel. The Committee had been entirely responsible and correctly so.

God certainly works in mysterious ways. We had been planning to leave Liverpool! D'rene and I went to Chinatown for a meal to sort out our thoughts ... it really was a celebration. I recall that the food that night was appalling, but, in spite of that, we decided that our future was in Liverpool.

When I was ever asked how I became Chaplain Superintendent of the Mersey Mission to Seamen, the only positive answer was that it had nothing to do with Chinese food!

The next move was a meeting with Clifford Martin, the Bishop of Liverpool. He asked to see me! He took off his wrist watch and placed it on the desk and sat back in his chair. I was poised on the edge of my nerves and seat. He addressed the ceiling.

"Tell me about the Mission as you see it and what you propose to do about it. You've got ten minutes and then we'll talk."

He folded his arms and seemed to retire into episcopal repose. I was on my own.

It had been easy to criticise. Most of us are superb at condemnation. If only his Lordship had asked about that, I could have waded in with gusto. Criticism is easy.

I probably said not much more than underlining the need to put the seafarer first. Years later, I still think that the work of a parson is just simply asking a man how he is and then listening to the answer.

So my world was turned upside down and I became a Chaplain Superintendent. The sea and the seafarer were to remain as the major thrust in my life for some thirty years. I had finally shaken the dust of Wales off my feet and transferred my dog collar to the docks. The Llandaff years were over ... without them I would not have survived in Liverpool.

Liverpool became my home.

# The Way to Liverpool

# The Way to Liverpool

The Way to Liverpool